The Matrix of Gog

The Matrix of Gog

Third Printing, 2024

 Published by RiverCrest Publishing, 4819 R.O. Drive, Suite 102, Spicewood, Texas 78669.

Cover design: Daniel Patrick

Printed in the United States of America

Library of Congress Catalog Card Number 2014931414

Categories: 1. Religion 2. Judaism 3. Science 4. History 5. Archaeology

ISBN 978-1-930004-83-2

The Matrix of Gog

DANIEL PATRICK

OTHER BOOKS BY RIVERCREST PUBLISHING

DNA Science and the Jewish Bloodline, by Texe Marrs

Conspiracy of the Six-Pointed Star, by Texe Marrs

Conspiracy World, by Texe Marrs

Mysterious Monuments: Encyclopedia of Secret Illuminati Designs, Masonic Architecture, and Occult Places, by Texe Marrs

Codex Magica: Secret Signs, Mysterious Symbols and Hidden Codes of the Illuminati, by Texe Marrs

Synagogue of Satan: The Secret History of Jewish World Domination, by Andrew Carrington Hitchcock

Protocols of the Learned Elders of Zion

Days of Hunger, Days of Chaos, by Texe Marrs

Project L.U.C.I.D.: The Beast 666 Universal Human Control System, by Texe Marrs

Circle of Intrigue: The Hidden Inner Circle of the Global Illuminati Conspiracy, by Texe Marrs

Dark Majesty: The Secret Brotherhood and the Magic of a Thousand Points of Light, by Texe Marrs

New Age Cults and Religions, by Texe Marrs

Mystery Mark of the New Age, by Texe Marrs

Dark Secrets of the New Age, by Texe Marrs

For additional information we highly recommend the following website:

www.powerofprophecy.com

TABLE OF Contents

INTRODUCTION

Matrix of Gog—The Fulfillment of Bible Prophecy

Ezekiel 38 and 39 are key to understanding the events of the last days. We read in Ezekiel that "Gog, from the land of Magog," a powerful world leader, will emerge. He and his military forces will descend on and conquer Israel and go on to precipitate a horrendous, deadly global war.

Who is "Gog," and where is "Magog?" Until recently, these vital questions were mysteries. But now, DNA science, history, and archeology have given us answers. Magog is the land of Khazaria, in the Caucasus, south of Russia. Gog, meanwhile, is the demonic leader, or king, of this great land.

Khazaria is the country of origin for today's "Jews," whom DNA science has confirmed are not descendants of Abraham and so, are not Israelites and Semites. The people whom we call "Jews" are, in fact, of the Turkic bloodline.

What this important book, *Matrix of Gog*, does is inform us about Gog, Magog, and the Jews. We discover that the Holy

Bible is accurate, that today's "Jews" are the "Synagogue of Satan" of *Revelation 2* and *3*.

Moreover, claiming to be Jews, the Khazars from Europe in recent decades have descended upon Israel in great numbers, just as prophesied. They have no family relationship and no ancestry to the ancient Israelites. As such, they are not the seed of Abraham but are pretenders. In an astonishing turn of events, today's "Jews" are, in reality, none other than followers of Gog, of the land of Magog.

—Texe Marrs, author
DNA Science and the Jewish Bloodline
Austin, TX 78733

PREFACE

The Matrix of GOG is aimed at one of the most naïve audiences that ever entered a church, so-called Christian Zionists. An alternate title could have been called: *What If ALL Your Bible Prophecy Supporting Zionist Israel Is Wrong?*

This prophetic delusion of Christian Zionists is not some obscure theological question posed by medieval monks such as "how many angels can dance on the head of a pin" but a world-wide political/economic issue that has already cost the lives of millions and stands ready to launch WW3.

Most Christian Zionists have their minds locked in to an unconditional support for the Israeli State by a prophetic paradigm that they believe is totally supported by Scripture. Here is a personal example of the consequences of this belief. Back in 1968, shortly after becoming a Christian, I was attending an evangelical church in Southern California. My pastor made the requisite pilgrimage to Israel to see firsthand the "fulfillment of prophecy" that he supposed was happening there. The only problem was that he ended up staying with a Palestinian Christian family to whom he became very attached.

One day, the father of the family asked him, "Why do American Christians support the Israelis who are destroying so many Christian Palestinians?" My pastor told me later that he was speechless at that question. He told me "I didn't know what to tell him, I really liked the Palestinian Christians I met and saw their plight but the reality is the prophecies are all against them."

Well, I'm here to tell you that the prophecies are not against the Palestinians. In fact, the favorite prophecy of the Christian Zionists about Gog and Magog in *Ezekiel, chapter 38 and 39,* is AGAINST the Zionists themselves.

So, if you happen to be one of the duped, as I was, I hope you have the guts to read on and have this "strong delusion" rooted out of your mind and spirit once and for all.

— Daniel Patrick

ONE

Who is GOG?

"The Word of the LORD came unto me, saying, Son of man, set thy face **against GOG**... and prophesy against him."

—*Ezekiel 38:1,2*

GOG is the force behind the creation of the worldwide money-power *Matrix* that we all live in today. Gog works with an international army of fanatics who have been colluding with governments for hundreds of years as money-lenders. At the beginning of the last century, Gog's army began to take total control of nations they invaded. Since 9/11, they have initiated the final stage in their war to conquer the entire planet, take over all governments and natural resources, and introduce their New World Order.

Their vision is to sit as elite monarchs over completely controlled, depopulated, enslaved subjects whose only function is to serve them. It will lead to the worst destruction the world has ever seen.

Now all this information about Gog is contained in the

ancient prophecy of Ezekiel, a prediction uttered nearly 2500 years ago. The prophet Ezekiel describes a war, initiated by someone called Gog, in which: *"all the men that are upon the face of the earth, shall shake...and the mountains (or kingdoms) shall be thrown down...and every wall shall fall to the ground" (Ezekiel 38:19,20).* Most of those who teach this tie it in with the prophecies found in the Book of Revelation and like to call it the Battle of Armageddon. It is said to be the final conflagration, holocaust, nuclear nightmare, worldwide earthquake, meteor strike, and destruction of all the kingdoms upon the earth, all rolled into one big shebang.

Millions believe the final fulfillment of this prophecy is just around the corner. If you think I'm exaggerating to freak you out, or fooling around with your mental space by trotting out ancient mumbo-jumbo believed by only a few dozen kooks—guess again. This end-time teaching is weekly Sunday sermon fodder for millions of churchgoers around the world. Books about it have sold by the multi-millions and dozens of movies and documentaries, both religious and Hollywood, portray the cataclysms described in this very same ancient prophecy.

Just flip through the religious TV channels and invariably the subject of Gog will come up almost every day. Though the televangelists often talk about this horrible Armageddon war that they believe is just ahead, usually, it's not about the coming war but how Christians need into support Gog and all the Gogsters and how the United States needs to send more military and economic support to Gog. So even if you don't believe in this stuff, they do!

They not only believe it but they are pouring **millions** of dollars of their **own** money into support of Gog, and are egging on their governments to give **billions** of dollars more in economic, and military support for Gog, and they are literally frothing at the mouth in anticipation for "Armageddon!" "Bring it on!," as one of their crazy leaders famously said.

Do you know what these whacky televangelists and preachers use to whip their congregations into a mad frenzy to support Gog and his army of fanatics, not only in the Middle-East but worldwide? Why they use these very same chapters of *Ezekiel 38 and 39!* The problem is, they have it all upside down and backwards, and they have ended up blessing Gog instead. You ask "How can this be?" They do it because of a total lack of understanding of who exactly Gog is.

These "Christian" Gogsters include John Hagee, Pat Robertson, Hal Lindsey, Chuck Smith, the Pope, God TV, TBN, the Baptists and about 90% of all Christian denominations. These guys are supposed to be Christians, and they say

Rev. John Hagee believes GOG is Russia. Wrong! He thinks GOG will lead a Moslem army against Israel. Wrong again! Here is Hagee, like millions of fellow Christian-Zionists, actually BLESSING GOG!

they believe in God and what He says in the Bible, yet here they are supporting Gog and blessing Gog and doing exactly the opposite of what God told the Prophet Ezekiel to do.

But you can hardly blame them, because the identity of **"GOG"** has been one of the greatest mysteries of all time. How can you prophesy against someone when you don't know who he is? If the Prophet Ezekiel was like most Christians today, I can just hear his response to God's command to *"prophesy against Gog"*—"OK LORD I'll do it!... But... uh... first, could you tell me—Who is GOG?"

That is a question that we all need an answer to. Why? First of all, because our understanding of who Gog is will help us not to be one of the duped who blindly follow blind preachers off the cliff, but one of those who see through the mass media manipulation and political propaganda of these charlatans. Secondly, it will help us to get ready for what is coming, because Gog and his army of fanatics are bringing about a war of such magnitude that it is going to tear our world apart!

So who is this "GOG?"

Ezekiel the Prophet calls GOG: the *"prince of Rosh, Meshech and Tubal"* from the *"land of Magog"* who, according to his prophecy in "*the latter years*" and "*the latter days,*" gathers "*a mighty army*" from "*many people*" and leads an invasion "*against the mountains of Israel.*"

The vast majority of Jewish and Christian teachers believe that this invasion of Gog and his army describes a **future** invasion of the nation of Israel, launched by either the Russians or the Arab/Moslem nations or both. From examining Jewish authorities and from intimate familiarity with evangelical Christian eschatology, I have to say that the majority of these have the identity of GOG all wrong. And because they have that wrong, their elaborate interpretations built on that error are wrong as well. This invasion is not off in the future but has already started and is fast approaching its cataclysmic end!

The first clue to discovering the identity of GOG is deciphering the name ***GOG*** itself. I don't want to prejudice the argument, as some might like to accuse me, so to avoid that, let's turn to a **Jewish source** to find out who the Jews themselves believe GOG is. The first source we go to is the Septuagint, translated from the Hebrew by 72 Jewish scholars over 300 years before Christ. The first quote below is from a modern translation of *Numbers 24:7* which was a prophecy against **Agag**. The second quote is also of *Numbers 24:7*, but from the Septuagint, that translated the same Hebrew word that most western Bibles render as **Agag**, but which they translated as **Gog**.

First, from the King James Version:

> ***Numbers 24:7*** *"his king shall be higher than* ***Agag****, and his kingdom shall be exalted."*

Now the Septuagint version:

> ***LXX version Numbers 24:7*** *"his kingdom will be lifted up above* ***Gog****, and his kingdom will be increased."*

Gog, according to the Septuagint, as seen in the above two verses, is **synonymous** with **Agag**. Agag is a generic term used for **kings of Amalek**. In Genesis it shows us that **Amalek** was the **grandson of Esau** who is also called **Edom**.

Jumping from ancient Jewish Bible translations, here is a modern internet Jewish source. This is from **"JAHG"** (Jews and Hasidic Gentiles), a Zionist web site, offering their proof that **Gog** is **Esau/Edom**.

> "I was extremely interested to read your article http://www.noahide.com/reds2.htm that mentioned the **'King of Gog/Amalek'**... If you don't mind, could you tell me the historical source that links the Amalekite **King Agag to 'Gog?'** I was unable to find a direct link in the Bible, so I wondered if there was another primary source for this link...."—Jeff in TX
>
> "**Our response:** The identity of King **Gog**...as descending from the seed of **Amalek** is alluded to in a variety of sources in the Jewish oral traditions. That **King Gog would be from the descendants of Esau/Edom** (which include **Amalek**) is mentioned in such sources as the **Targum of Yonasan ben Uziel** on Isaiah 11:4, **Bereishis Rabba 76:5**, and others. This specifically means Amalek, as implied by the Lubavitcher Rebbe (e.g., **Likkutei Sichos** 1, **Parshas Yisro, no. 9**)." (http://www.noahide.com/newsletter/news03.htm)

Here's another Jewish site called "**Ask Moses**" that affirms the Septuagint rendering of Agag for Gog:

> "The **Septuagint** identifies **Agag** with **Gog**.... Agag is a generic name for the kings of Amalek... Amalek is a tribe descended from Esau." (www.askmoses.com).

These Jewish internet sites referring to their own ***"Jewish oral tradition"*** show that they believe **Gog** is **Agag** and how the Septuagint identifies the name **Agag** as **Gog**. They also point out the fact that **Agag** was the **King of Amalek**, who is part of **Edom**. Besides the Septuagint, other Bible translations including the Samaritan Pentateuch, Old Latin, Modern English, Moffat, Aquila Bible and other versions also translate **"Agag"** as **"Gog."**

TO REVIEW: GOG is **synonymous** with **AGAG**—**AGAG** is the **TITLE** of the **King of the Amalekites/ Edomites**—just as Pharaoh was the title of the leader of Egypt or Czar the title of the leader of Russia. We first hear of Agag in *Numbers 24:7* during the time of Moses. Then, centuries after *Numbers* was written, we read that during the reign of King Saul the Prophet Samuel slew *"Agag, king of the Amalekites" (1 Samuel 15:32)*. This shows us that Agag was a title passed down to the kings of Amalek/Edom. And, as we will show you later, this guy is still around today, only not where you'd expect him to be, and he will show up in **your** future!

The next clue to GOG's identity really lies in identifying over who exactly does Ezekiel's prophecy predict that GOG/ AGAG will be the ***"prince"*** or *ruler*? Now, this is where it gets a little eerie because the Prophet now says that this GOG, this AGAG, this king of EDOM from a little tribe in ancient Palestine, is going to be the prince or ruler of *"Ros, Meshech and Tubal."* These are ancient names for Moscow, Tobolsk and Russia. Now that is quite a journey no matter how you figure it.

So, let's look at the original prophecy. Several modern English translations of *Ezekiel* follow the King James Version (KJV), and translate the Hebrew to read that "Gog" is the "***CHIEF*** prince of Meshech and Tubal." Other translations render Gog as the "prince of ***ROSH/ROS***, Meshech and Tubal." The controversy centers on whether the Hebrew word ***"rosh"*** should be *translated* or *transliterated.* To *translate* is to give the meaning of a word in another language. To *transliterate* means to bring the phonics, or the way a word sounds, into another language. Transliteration is usually done with peoples names, or names of places, countries etc.

The Hebrew word ***"rosh"*** in the Old Testament is usually translated as a common noun such as **chief**, leader, head, highest, etc. Because **"rosh"** is basically identical to **"Rus/ Rosh/Rhos,"** old names for the country of **Russia**, some say that *transliterating* "rosh" as a proper name is trying to make the Bible fit your interpretation of so-called "end-time" prophecy.

However, in 300 BC, the 72 Jewish translators of the Old Testament into Greek (called the *Septuagint*) didn't have any end-time theology to push and they transliterated "rosh" as a proper noun, as a **name**: "Gog, prince of **Rosh**, Meshech, and Tubal."

Dr. John Thomas, who wrote ***"Gogue and Magogue"*** in 1848, tells us that the Septuagint translators:

> *"Were sensible, that in this place it was not an appellative [or common] noun, but a proper name; and they rendered it accordingly by Ros. But Jerome [who translated the Old Testament into Latin], not finding any such proper name among the nation-families mentioned in Genesis, rather disputed the Septuagint reading, and preferred to consider the word* ***Ros*** *as a common noun [chief]; and his interpretation, established in the Latin Vulgate, has universally prevailed throughout the west. Jerome, however, was more*

> *scrupulous than the editors of later versions, who have unqualifiedly rejected it as a proper name; for although he inclined to the other rendering, he did not feel authorized to reject altogether one so ancient, and he has therefore preserved them both, translating the passage thus—"Gogue, terram, Magogue, principem capitis (sive **Ros**) Mosoch et Thubal."*

Thomas further reveals that Ros or Rosh is the root word for Russia:

> *"[The historian] Bochart, about the year 1640, observed in his elaborate researches into Sacred Geography, that **Ros** is the most ancient form under which history makes mention of the name of **RUSSIA**; and he contended that ...the **Russian nation** was **called Ros by the Greeks** in the earliest period in which we find it mentioned. The **Ros** are a Scythian nation, bordering on the northern Taurus. And their **own** historians say, 'It is related that the **Russians** (whom the Greeks called **Ros**, and sometimes Rosos) derived their name from Ros, a valiant man, who delivered his nation from the yoke of their tyrants.'*
>
> *It is not difficult to recognize in **Tobl**, Tubl, or Thobel, a name which naturally connects itself with... the river **Tobol** which gives name to the city **Tobolium**, or **Tobolski** the metropolis of the extensive region of Siberia."*

Etymology is the study of the origin of words. We find as

far back as the Septuagint in 300 BC the name **Ros/Rosh** as a proper noun, in other words, the name of a geographical country. We also find historians throughout history who viewed Ezekiel's *"Rosh, Meshech and Tubal"* as the **origin** of the word **Russia, Moscow and Tobolsk**. Bear in mind that these ancient writers had no particular end-time prophecy scenarios to propagate either. Meshech, Tubal and Magog are mentioned in *Genesis, chapter 10* as descendants of Japheth, one of the three sons of Noah. *"The sons of Japheth: Gomer and **Magog** and Madai and Javan and **Tubal** and **Meshech**."* Ros/Rosh, Meshech, Tubal and Magog are ancient names whose descendants settled the land area of modern Russia.

It is generally surmised by many Bible scholars that Russia will sometime in the future launch a massive invasion against the modern state of Israel. Well, at least that was the popular prediction until 1987 when the old Soviet empire ostensibly fell apart. Then the scholars looked to Iraq, and now they theorize Iran and even China. But they are way off base, as we will show. This invasion is not off in the future but commenced when Gog became the prince or ruler of Russia. That was on November 7, 1917, which we will go into great detail to explain in chapter 5 and which is why I number this clue as number 6.

I believe the **key** to deciphering this prophecy lies in finding out the true identity of **GOG**. The Lord says to *"set your face against Gog and prophesy against him... and say Thus saith the Lord God, I am against thee."* Most of the prophecy "experts" have fingered the wrong guy as Gog and have therefore been letting the real culprit slip away. And because they have the identity of Gog all wrong they have a twisted interpretation for this prophecy as well.

Both ancient and modern Jewish authorities say Gog is synonymous with Agag, king of Amalek and Edom, old biblical names that don't mean much to the average person today. So here's a little history lesson: The Old Testament patriarch **Abraham** had a son, **Isaac,** who had a set of twins: **Esau** and **Jacob**. Jacob's name was later changed to **Israel** and he had 12 sons who became the 12 tribes of Israel who colonized the land of Palestine around 1450 BC. The name Israel was later used in the Bible to describe the **northern 10 tribes** who were also sometimes called **Ephraim**, who was the **grandson** of **Jacob/Israel**.

The name **Judah**, from which we get the word **Jew**, was used to denote the southern two tribes of Judah and Benjamin and their Levites or priests. **Esau**, Jacob's twin brother, also had a name change. He was sometimes called Edom which means red in Hebrew. Esau also had several sons who became know as **Edomites** who were later called **Idumeans** by the Greeks.

Amalek was Esau's **grandson**. Just as Ephraim, Jacob's grandson, became head of a leading tribe in Israel, so Amalek became the leading tribe of Esau/**Edom**. **Agag** was the king of the **Amalekites**. As we said, Agag is **not** someone's **name**, it is a **title**, like **king**, or **czar**. **Agag** was the ruler of the **Edomite** tribe of **Amalek**.

The main thing you need to fix in your mind from all of this, is that **'Gog'** is synonymous with **'Agag'** and that **Agag** is the **King of Edom/Amelek**. And that understanding brings us to our *first clue* on the **identity** of **Gog**:

Gog *is* ***Agag,*** *king of* ***Edom/Amalek****.*

TWO

Gog, Agag, and Edom/Amalek

FIRST CLUE—The Septuagint translators of 300 BC give us our first clue in learning the identity of Gog. We find out from these translators of 2300 years ago that **Gog is called Agag** and that Ezekiel prophesied 2500 years ago that he will be the ruler of Rosh/Russia, Meshech/Moscow, Tubal/Tobolsk and Magog, the land area of Eastern Europe. That is a journey of thousands of years and thousands of miles. Now we follow the trail to see how he went from the deserts of Palestine to take control of Russia and create the world-wide money matrix we all live in today.

Gog/Agag is the **king of Amalek/Edom**. Most Israeli Jews, and many Christians, identify all the Arabs and Palestinians, in fact ALL the enemies of Jews or the state of Israel as Amalek and Edom! They view them as Edomite enemies who must be annihilated so Israel can possess their "promised land" or "eretz Israel," all the land from the Nile river to the Euphrates river. Their view couldn't be further from the truth.

Herod Antipas, an Edomite, beheaded John the Baptist and conspired with Pilate in Jesus' crucifixion. These Edomites are still around today and are still the enemies of Christ.

Since Agag is the king of Edom/Amelek, if we could find **Edom**, then we could find Gog. Where is **Edom** today? Where is **Amalek** today? Where is **Agag** today? Where is **GOG** today? I'll tell you where he is at, Gog is hiding in the **synaGOGue**!

Here is how Gog got there. According to the Jewish historian Josephus, who wrote around 70-95 AD, the Jewish, Maccabean leader, John Hyrcanus conquered Edom in 126 BC:

> *"**Hyrcanus** took also Dora and Marissa, cities of **Idumea** [the Greek word for **Edom**], and subdued all the Idumeans; and permitted them to stay in that country, if they would circumcise their genitals, and make use of the laws of the Jews;*

> *and they were so desirous of living in the country of their forefathers, that they submitted to the use of* ***circumcision****, and the rest of the Jewish ways of living; at which time therefore this befell them, that* ***they were hereafter none other than Jews****" (Antiquities of the Jews Chapter IX).*

Referring to Josephus' quote above, a Baptist magazine sheds some light:

> *"William Whiston, translator of Josephus, adds this note: 'This account of the* ***Idumeans [Edomites]*** *admitting circumcision, and the entire Jewish law "from this time," or from the days of Hyrcanus, is confirmed by their entire history afterwards. This, in the opinion of Josephus, made them proselytes of justice, or entire Jews" (Illinois and Indiana Missionary Baptist, January 2001).*

Some Bible commentators believe that Edom was wiped out and totally disappeared from history. But history, as recorded by Josephus, shows us that **Edom/Amalek/Agag/ Gog** did **not** disappear from history. No! They disappeared **into Jewry** as Josephus tells us; and that from the time of their conquest by John Hyrcanus in 126 BC and forward: ***"they were hereafter none other than Jews."***

SECOND CLUE—Gog/Agag, together with Edom, absorbed into Jewry.

Our second clue to the identity of Gog is that **Gog/Agag,** along with his Edomites, were absorbed into Jewry beginning in **126 BC.**

This is confirmed again by *The Jewish Encyclopedia,* 1925

edition, Vol. 5, p. 41, which says, *"**Edom** is **in** modern **Jewry**."*

But the Edomites proved to be a tricky bunch, for less than a hundred years after their defeat by the Maccabees and absorption into Jewry, Gog/Agag/Edom, in the form of the **Herodian** dynasty, became **King of the Jews!** Herod and his descendants were all **Edomites**. Remember **King Herod** from your Christmas stories? He's the one who had all the young male children killed in order to try and kill Jesus as a child. His son, **Herod Antipas**, conspired with Pontus Pilate in the crucifixion of Jesus. The grandson, **Herod Agrippa I**, persecuted the early Christians and had James the brother of John executed. **Herod Agrippa II** presided over Paul the apostle's trial.

Herod the Great was officially given the title ***King of Judaea*** by the Roman Empire in 37 BC—he was the King of the Jews. His wife, Mariamne, was a Jew and descendant of the **Maccabees**. Herod the Edomite, as **king,** was really

Followers of King Herod, shown here killing the babies, are still around today. Herod was an Edomite and became King of the Jews in 37 BC.

fulfilling the **role** of **Agag**. Herod was Agag/Gog, a King of Edom.

But Gog is more than just a flesh and blood king. As we shall see, Gog is both the physical manifestation of the king and the **demon** spirit behind the throne. The demon inhabits the man and propels him to the title of Gog/Agag/King.

The Babylonian Talmud is the Scripture-twisting *"leaven of the Pharisees"* Jesus warned against *(Matthew 16:6)*. It was codified under the dark influences of Babylon. It is the *"curse that goes forth over ALL the Earth" (Zechariah 5:3)*.

This is very biblical. Remember what Satan told Jesus? *"ALL these kingdoms are mine and to whomsoever I will I give it."* And in the Book of *Revelation* we find: *"The Dragon (Satan) gave him (the King) his power and seat (throne) and great authority" (Revelation 13:2).*

The demonic spiritual realm, according to Scripture, is hierarchical with demonic powers under Satan ruling over different territories. These demonic spirits empower and use people to control the kingdoms of this world.

Paul the Apostle called Satan the *"spirit that works in the children of disobedience."* And he says that as Christians our fight is *"not against flesh and blood, but against principalities, against powers, against the rulers of the darkness of this world, against spiritual wickedness in high places" (Ephesians 6:12).* Since all political and religious opposition to Christ is obviously flesh and blood, by contrast it's also obvious that the "powers and principalities" that Paul is referring to here are not flesh and blood but spiritual forces of Satan. One of the greatest of these demonic forces is GOG.

Gog, as the ruler of the Edomite tribe of Amalek, was one of the original, implacable foes of God's people in the Old Testament. The Bible prophesies that God's people will have perpetual *"war with Amalek from generation to generation."* This war has never ceased.

This demonic *"principality"* of Gog entered Jewry in 126 BC when John Hyrcanus conquered all the Edomites and they converted to Judaism. Just to show you how powerful Gog is, it only took him a few decades to maneuver an Edomite king to be the ruler of the Jews and become the murderer of Christ in collusion with the Jews. And it was the descendants of Herod, along with the rejecting Jews, who became the first persecutors and murderers of Christ's followers. That demonic force is still within worldwide Jewry today.

This demonic side of Gog is clearly seen in another verse from the Old Testament Prophet, Amos, *"Thus the Lord showed me, and behold a swarm of locusts were coming, and behold, one of the young devastating* ***locusts*** *was* ***Gog****, the* ***King****." Amos 7:1 (Septuagint)*

This *"swarm of Locusts"* has to be symbolic for in *Proverbs 30:27* it says that *"the locusts have* ***NO King****."*

However, in the Book of Revelation, we encounter another swarm of locusts that come up from the ***"Abyss"*** that **do have a KING** over them called **Abaddon** or **Apollyon**, the **Destroyer**:

> *"And out of the smoke locusts came down upon the earth and were given power like that of scorpions of the earth. They were told not to harm the grass of the earth or any plant or tree, but only those people who did not have the seal of God on their foreheads.*

> *They were not given power to kill them, but only to torture them for five months. And the agony they suffered was like that of the sting of a scorpion when it strikes a man. During those days men will seek death, but will not find it; they will long to die, but death will elude them. The* ***locusts*** *looked like horses prepared for battle. On their heads they wore something like crowns of gold, and their faces resembled human faces. Their hair was like women's hair, and their teeth were like lions' teeth. They had breastplates like breastplates of iron, and the sound of their wings was like the thundering of many horses and chariots rushing into battle. They had tails and stings like scorpions, and in their tails they had power to torment people for five months. They had as king over them, the angel of the Abyss, whose name in Hebrew is Abaddon, and in Greek, Apollyon" (Revelation 9:3-11).*

These "locusts" you won't find in any biology book! They are symbolic of the demonic forces of Satan who torment the people who are not sealed with the Holy Spirit of God. In Amos we find that Gog is leading this army of locusts and in the Revelation the "angel of the Abyss" called Abaddon or the Destroyer is leading them. They are obviously one and the same.

These verses from *Ezekiel*, *Amos*, and *Revelation* show that Gog is both a spiritual entity as well as a human incarnation of that demonic force. The **spiritual** forces behind the earthly representations are where the **real** power lies. These unseen forces are the real "**powers** behind the **throne**" of the kings of this world. They embody and empower GOG himself.

As Bob Dylan said: *"You Gotta Serve Somebody—It may*

be the Devil or it may be the Lord, but you gotta serve somebody." When *"the Jews killed the Lord Jesus and their own prophets"* as the apostle Paul said, the only alternative left was Gog. And Gog became the prince of worldwide Jewry.

THIRD CLUE—GOG/AGAG is King of the Jews

That is our third clue, Gog/Agag the King of Edom. Beginning with Herod, Gog/Agag became King of the Jews. Remember what the Jews cried out after Pontius Pilate had scourged Jesus and he presented Him to the Jewish mob, declaring "Behold your King?" They said "Crucify him! We have no king but Caesar!"

Since the Herodian dynasty had been appointed by Caesar, this is probably when the spirit of Gog took control of the Jewish hierarchy. This does not mean that every leader that Gog empowers will have the official title "King of the Jews." In fact, after their destruction and dispersion by the Romans, it took centuries for the Jews to become organized enough to have anything like a central authority. But all the while, Gog was in their midst as a spiritual force using different individuals and groups to bring about his will.

Gog the demon also doesn't have to be bound to one person. You can see this in the way that Satan himself operated to oppose the ministry of Jesus. One time Satan appears to Jesus tempting him at the end of his 40 day fast (see *Luke 4*). Another time, Satan spoke right through Peter's own mouth which earned him the rebuke by Jesus, "Get thee behind me Satan!" Finally, Satan entered in to Judas and accomplished Jesus' betrayal and murder. I'm sure Satan was also in some of those Jewish leaders too, since Jesus said they were of their father the Devil *(John 8:44)* so I am sure that Gog operates the same way.

What happens to Gog next? Well, in 70 AD the Roman

legions conquered and destroyed the city of Jerusalem. Josephus records that 20,000 Edomites came to fight alongside the Jewish Zealots in their losing battle against the Romans. Tens of thousands of Jews and Edomites were killed in the fight. The vanquished were crucified by the thousands, many were sold into slavery and the rest fled into the countryside.

The Jews/Edomites were bloody but unbowed, for 60 years later under Bar Kochba they fought the Romans again —and were defeated again. This time Rome passed a law forbidding any Jews to live in Judea. The remaining Jews/ Edomites fled to pre-existent Jewish colonies in Egypt and Babylon.

With all the Jewish genealogical records destroyed by the Romans, the Jews and Edomites became thoroughly integrated into one body. The Edomites didn't become Jews in the sight of God at that time either, but the Jews who rejected Christ became like Edomites instead. How is that? The Jews that rejected Christ lost their birthright as "the chosen" just like the firstborn son Esau/Edom had lost his birthright to his twin brother Jacob back in the Old Testament. Jesus told them "the Kingdom of God shall be taken from you," and Paul said these were the "natural branches that were broken off" (*Matthew 21:43; Romans 11:17-24*). If you don't follow the "King of the Jews," Jesus Christ, who is the "King of Israel" you are neither a Jew nor part of Israel no matter what you think your natural genealogy is. Period.

The "Edomite-Jews" who fled into Egypt later migrated into Spain and became known as **Sephardim**, Sepharad being Hebrew for **Spain**. Those in Babylon later became known as **Ashkenazim**. These today, are the two main branches of Judaism, with the Ashkenazi outnumbering the Sephardic at least 10 to 1. Ever wonder how the Ashkenazi became more populous than the Sephardic? Probably not—but we will show you anyway, since it's important in finding out the identity of Gog today.

There in Babylon the Edomite-Jews codified their "oral tradition" into what became known as the **Babylonian Talmud**, a book, according to the Rabbis, which takes precedence over the Torah, and the rest of the Tanach, which together Christians call the Old Testament. This *"oral tradition"* is what caused Jesus in the Gospel of *Matthew, chapter 15* and *23* to state, *"Ye serpents, ye generation of vipers... by your* ***traditions*** *ye make* **void** *the law of God."* Read both chapters and don't miss *John, chapter 8* while you are at it "*Ye are of your Father the devil, he was a liar from the beginning and abode not in the truth because there is no truth in him."*

Be careful about the Talmud! I believe this book is what the Prophet Zechariah referred to as recorded in the fifth chapter of his prophecy as a "**scroll, or book, of oppression, lies and false balances** which unclean birds, or spirits, carried to the land of Shinar (Babylon) where they built a house for it." He called it "the curse which goes forth over the **WHOLE** earth" *(vs 3)*—and it has! It is this book called the Babylonian Talmud that is the holy book of worldwide Jewry today and what is taught in all the rabbinical schools (yeshivas) around the world. (Check out Appendix Two for some quotes from the Talmud about Jesus and Mary his mother and about Gentiles in general. It's an eye-opener).

THREE

Gog and the "House of Togarmah"—The Khazars

> "I will bring thee (Gog) forth, and all thine army…the house of Togarmah of the north quarters, and all his bands: and many people with thee."
>
> —*Ezekiel 38:4,6*

After their expulsion from Judea in 70AD and again in 126AD, many Edomite-Jews settled in pre-existent Jewish colonies in Babylon (modern Baghdad in Iraq) and Constantinople (modern Istanbul). It was from these rabbinical schools in Babylon and Byzantium that the Edomite-Jews sent proselytizers to the King of Khazaria around 740 AD. This led to the Khazarian empire converting to Talmudic Judaism. This story is related in the *Jewish Encyclopedia* and is beyond refute. In the 1970s Arthur Koestler, himself an Ashkenazi Jew, and author of over 25 books and essays, published his indepth research into this conversion in a book he rather tongue-in-cheek called *The*

Arthur Koestler, author of the book, *The Thirteenth Tribe*.

Thirteenth Tribe—a pun on the twelve tribes of Israel in the Bible, with the Khazarian nation becoming the thirteenth tribe of Israel. Koestler showed how this conversion of multitudes of Khazars into Judaism swelled the ranks of the Ashkenazi Jews. And guess what? The Khazars weren't even Semites! They were not descended from Shem but descended through Japheth and his son Magog. None of their forefathers had even put a toe in the "promised land."

The history of this Khazar conversion to Judaism is recorded in many Jewish, Christian and Arab sources. Koestler's book includes the 10th century correspondence between Joseph the King, or Khagan, of Khazaria and Hasdai Ibn Shaprut of Cordova, a Jewish doctor and foreign minister to the court of Sultan Abdu al-Rahm, the Caliph of Spain. The letters were first published by the Jews themselves in 1577. Koestler records how the rabbi, Judah Halevi, knew of the letters even in 1140.

Koestler's book relates the story of how, around 930 AD,

Hasdai Ibn Shaprut became aware of a Jewish nation north of the Caucusus mountains through merchants from the region coming to Spain and decided to send letters back with them to the Kagan of Khazaria to find the truth of the matter. Shaprut thought that maybe they were some of the lost tribes of Israel that had gone into Assyrian captivity in 722 BC, and asked the Khagan if this was the case. Khagan Joseph responded that they were not the lost tribes of Israel but had descended through **Khazar,** son of **Togarmah**, son of **Magog**, son of **Japheth**. This meant that they had **no Semitic bloodline** at all for the Semites trace their genealogy through **Shem** the brother of Japheth.

Here is how Koestler relates the reply from King Joseph of Khazaria to Hasdai Ibn Shaprut:

> "**Joseph** then proceeds to provide a genealogy of his people. Though a fierce Jewish nationalist, proud of wielding the "scepter of Judah," he cannot, and does not, claim for them Semitic descent; he traces their ancestry **not to Shem**, but to Noah's third son, **Japheth**; or more precisely to Japheth's grandson, **Togarma**, the ancestor of all Turkish tribes. "We have found in the family registers of our fathers," Joseph asserts boldly, "that Togarma had ten sons, and the names of their offspring are as follows: Uigur, Dursu, Avars, Huns, Basilii, Tarniakh, **Khazars**, Zagora, Bulgars, Sabir. We are the sons of **Khazar**, the seventh…"

This is rather amazing, since Koestler points out that the majority of Jews in the world, the Ashkenazi, who compose about 90% of worldwide Jewry, owe their great population advantage over the Sephardic Jews due to this great influx of

probably half a million Khazar Turks converting to Judaism. This has got to be one of the greatest ironies in history. For not only are the Ashkenazi the loudest voices screaming anti-Semitism, they are the one who initiated political Zionism to 'return' to the 'promised land'—a land in which the majority of their forefathers never even had put one toe in!

Benjamin Freedman who is an Ashkenazi Jew and convert to Christianity, knowing of this historical irony, put it this way concerning the Jews "return" to their so-called "promised land:"

> "There wasn't one of them who had an ancestor who ever put a toe in the Holy Land. Not only in Old Testament history, but also back to the beginning of time. Not one of them! And yet they come to the Christians and ask us to support their

> armed insurrections in Palestine by saying, "You want to help repatriate God's 'Chosen People' to their 'Promised Land,' their ancestral home, don't you? It's your Christian duty. We gave you one of our boys as your Lord and Savior. You now go to church on Sunday, and you kneel and you worship a Jew, and we're Jews."
>
> But they are pagan Khazars who were converted just the same as the Irish were converted [to Christianity]. It is as ridiculous to call them "people of the Holy Land," as it would be to call the 54 million Chinese Moslems Arabs." (This is online at various sites—Google it.)
>
> —*Benjamin Freedman Speaks*

Writing between 930 and 956 AD, Khagan Joseph of Khazaria relates the story of the Khazar conversion to Jewry in 740 AD thusly:

> "Khagan Bulan came to the conclusion that paganism is useless. 'It is shameful for us to be pagans. Let us adopt one of the heavenly religions, Christianity, Judaism or Islam.' So Bulan summoned three priests representing the three religions and had them dispute their creeds before him. But, no priest could convince the others, or the sovereign, that his religion was the best. So the ruler spoke to each of them separately. He asked the Christian priest: 'if you were not a Christian or had to give up Christianity, which would you prefer—Islam or Judaism? The priest said: If I were to give up

> Christianity, I would become a Jew. Bulan then asked the follower of Islam the same question, and the Moslem also chose Judaism. This is how Bulan came to choose Judaism for himself and the people of Khazaria in the seventh century AD and thereafter the Khazars (sometimes spelled Chazars and Khozars) lived according to Judaic laws."

Khagan Joseph goes on to tell how later under the rule of Khagan Obadiah, Judaism gained further strength in Khazaria. Synagogues and schools were built to give instruction in the Jewish religion. This immersion into Talmudic Judaism is also recorded by **Professor Graetz** in his ***"History of the Jews:"***

> "A successor of Bulan who bore the Hebrew name of Obadiah was the first to make serious efforts to further the Jewish religion. He invited Jewish sages to settle in his dominions, rewarded them royally... and introduced a divine service modeled on the ancient communities. After Obadiah came a long series of Jewish Chagans (Khagans), for according to a fundamental law of the state only Jewish rulers were permitted to ascend the throne."

Khazars and Arab Moslem armies fought wars for over 200 years. The Khazars, according to Arab chroniclers, were able to place as many as three hundred thousand soldiers in some of their battles. The Khazars ruled the entire area above the Caucasus mountains taking tribute from all the tribes of the Steppes and from all merchant caravans.

They controlled the Volga passes between the Black and

Caspian seas. Described by their enemies as ferocious warriors, almost like demons from hell, who used the skulls of their enemies as drinking cups and their scalps as napkins. They butchered and killed more people than the Black Plague. The size and power of the Kingdom of Khazaria is indicated by the fact that it sent an army of 40,000 soldiers (in 626-627) to help Heraclius of the Byzantines to conquer the Persians. *The Jewish Encyclopedia* proudly refers to Khazaria as having had a "well constituted and **tolerant** government (these are the same characters who also wrote that Stalin had a tolerant government too), a flourishing trade and a well-disciplined army."

Koestler, faced with the overwhelming evidence of the Khazar/Jewish connection, seems to arrive at some type of Orwellian 'doublethink' to rationalize the present Israeli state in his own mind. He says even though the Israeli state bases its existence on an historical tie to Biblical Israel that turns out to be a total illusion, that even so, the Zionist state should exist simply because now it is there.

Koestler was not a religious Jew but he never abandoned his Jewish secular identity, though he was honest enough to admit it's **illusionary 'chosen people' history**. His book should be on every Christian pastor's desk as a reference to wake them out of their own illusion and delusion about the so-called 'chosen people' and their 'return' to a 'Promised Land' that was never promised to any of the ancestors of these Khazars or Edomites in the first place.

One book that predated Koestler's on the Khazar origin of Ashkenazi Jews was by the Professor of Medieval Jewish History at Tel Aviv University, A. N. Poliak. His book, ***Khazaria,*** was published in 1944 in Tel Aviv, and a second edition in 1951. Poliak's book is considered even more radical than Koestler's by detractors. It was only published in Hebrew and created quite a storm throughout Jewry by challenging the "chosen people" thesis on which the Israeli nation is based. In his introduction he writes that, "the facts demand a new approach, both to the problem of the relations between the Khazar Jewry and other Jewish communities, and to the question of how far we can go in regarding this [Khazar] Jewry as the nucleus of the large Jewish settlement in Eastern Europe....since the descendants of this settlement—constitute now the large majority of world Jewry."

To Zionists, these revealing books on the origins of Ashkenazi Jewry are like a Frankenstein nightmare that just won't die no matter how many times they try to kill it in their media. It was revived again by another truth-seeking Ashkenazi Jew in a 1993 book, ***The Ashkenazic 'Jews:' A Slavo-Turkic People in Search of a Jewish Identity*** (Slavica Publishers), by Dr. Paul Wexler, a Tel Aviv University linguist. The title alone, is enough to make most Zionists brains go into "shock and awe."

One critic summarized Wexler's book in this short paragraph: "Wexler uses a reconstruction of Yiddish to argue that it began as a Slavic language whose vocabulary was largely replaced with German words. Going even further, he contends that the Ashkenazic Jews are predominantly converted **Slavs** and **Turks** who merged with a tiny population of **Palestinian Jews** from the Diaspora."

There are several other books out there on the subject as well. Koestler's book, and references to it, are all over the internet. If you search diligently, you may be able to find it in its entirety just waiting to be copied, or buy it on Amazon and give away copies to your favorite "Christian" Zionist. So the truth is there for those who wish to see it, but if not they can always stand on the scripture: *"The god of this world (Satan), hath blinded the minds of them which believe not" (2 Corinthians 4:4).* After all, it's much easier to believe a lie.

FOURTH CLUE—The house of Togarmah/Khazar/ Ashkenazi Jews teams up with GOG

This brings us to our fourth clue. Gog/Agag/Edom/Jewry is teamed up with the Khazars, who, as King Joseph reveals in his letter, are from the lineage of Togarmah, or as Ezekiel says, the "**house** of **Togarmah.**"

By the year 1000 AD there had been Jews living in Babylon, now called Baghdad, for nearly 1600 years—ever since 586 BC and the destruction of Jerusalem by Nebuchadnezzar and his army who destroyed Jerusalem and took as captive thousands of Jews as slaves to his city kingdom of Babylon. Around 516 BC some Jews returned to Judea and **rebuilt** their temple and city Jerusalem. Later, in 70 AD and again in 126 AD, Jews, along with their Jewish/Edomite/Gog/ Agag converts, fled the Roman destruction of the rebuilt Jerusalem and joined their Jewish brethren in Baghdad/ Babylon. Other Jews from Palestine found refuge in the eastern Roman capital of Constantinople in Byzantium.

Because of various 'persecutions' against the Jews at these Muslim and Christian capitals, some Jews left Babylon/ Bagdad and Byzantium seeking refuge in the Kingdom of Khazaria. There they all became one, big, happy **Ashkenazi** family helping to set up Talmud/Yeshiva schools and synagogues through out the land and further cementing the Khazars into the Jewish religion. As Jesus said to the Pharisees *"Ye compass land and sea to make one proselyte, and when he is made, ye make him twofold more the child of hell than yourselves" (Matthew 23:15).* Two hundred years later, in the 1200s, whatever original Judaic blood may have been in the inhabitants of Judea of the first century, it was now thoroughly mixed with two huge blood transfusions. The first from their Edomite relatives in 126 BC and the second from Khazarian converts, the non-semitic, children of Japheth, starting in 740 AD.

This brings us up to the middle of the 12th century, and that's when Genghis Khan and His bloodthirsty Golden Hordes arrived on the scene. Khan's armies drove the Khazars from the Steppes and into Russia and Eastern Europe.

Before the invasion of Genghis Khan, the Khazars already had small enclaves in Eastern Europe and Russia, most notably in Kiev which many historians believe was first settled by the Khazars. But with the arrival of Khan's armies the Khazar emigration trickle into these countries turned into a flood. Koestler shows, with meticulous documentation, how only this influx of Khazar multitudes can account for the sudden appearance in Eastern Europe of tens of thousands of 'Jews' at this time.

Historian and author Michael A. Hoffman II of RevisionistHistory.org has unearthed a photo of a Ukrainian statue depicting "Ukrainian Prince Sviatoslav's defeat of the Khazar army, 968 A.D. (note the hexagram on the Khazar soldier's shield)." According to Hoffman, "The Magen David was used in Jewish Kabbalistic rituals in the Middle Ages, but only became universally 'Jewish' in the 19th century when adopted by the Zionist movement as their national symbol: the misnamed 'Star of David,' which it most definitely is not."

The defeat by the Russians led to a reduction in Khazar sovereignty, but it wasn't until the arrival of Genghis Khan's armies in the 1200s that the Khazar mass migration into Eastern Europe began.

Koestler relates:

> "Polish historian, Adam Vetulani [writes] 'Polish scholars agree that these oldest settlements [in Poland] were founded by Jewish emigres from

This photo is of a statue that was in the Ukraine depicting the Ukrainian victory over the Khazars in 968 A.D. Note the so-called 'Star of David' on the shield of the Khazar soldier. Khazar = Jew!

> the Khazar state and Russia, while the Jews from Southern and Western Europe [Sephardic] began to arrive and settle only later… and that a certain proportion at least of the Jewish population (in earlier times, the main bulk) originated from the east, from the Khazar country, and later from Kievian Russia.'"

Koestler then shows how massive this immigration had to have been:

> "This leads us to the question of the approximate size and composition of the Khazar immigration into Poland. Regarding the numbers involved, we have no reliable information to guide us. We remember that the Arab sources speak of Khazar armies numbering three hundred thousand men involved in the Muslim-Khazar wars between 740 and 900 AD; and even if allowance is made for quite wild exaggerations, this would indicate a total Khazar population of at least half a million souls."

Koestler further documents that ONLY the Khazars can account for the huge numbers of Ashkenazi Jews in Eastern Europe:

> "The traditional conception of Jewish historians that the Crusade of 1096…or that the Black Plague of the mid 1200s…swept like a broom a mass migration of German Jews into Poland is simply a legend—or rather an *ad hoc* hypothesis invented because, as they knew little of Khazar history, they could see no other way to account for the emergence, out of nowhere, of this unprecedented concentration of Jews in Eastern Europe."

The reality, as Koestler and many historians document, was that there were only very small numbers of Jews who had communities in Germany, France, Holland and England. These were Jews from the Diaspora of Pre-Roman and Roman times who had been joined by Sephardic Jews after they had been expelled from Spain at the end of the fifteenth century.

I also agree with Koestler that:

> "It would, of course, be foolish to deny that Jews of different origin also contributed to the existing Jewish world community. The numerical ratio of the Khazar to the Semitic and other contributions is impossible to establish. But the cumulative evidence makes one inclined to agree with the consensus of Polish historians that "in earlier times the main bulk originated from the Khazar country;" and that, accordingly, the Khazar contribution to the genetic make-up of the Jews must be substantial, and in all likelihood dominant."

The census that took place just before Koestler wrote his book reveals that:

> "In the 1960s the number of Sephardim was estimated at 500,000. The Ashkenazim, at the same period, numbered about eleven million. Thus, in common parlance, Jew is practically synonymous with Ashkenazi Jew. But the term is misleading, for the Hebrew word Ashkenaz was, in mediaeval rabbinical literature, applied to Germany—thus contributing to the legend that modern Jewry originated on the Rhine. There is, however, no other term to refer to the non-Sephardic majority of contemporary Jewry. For the sake of piquantry [stimulating dissension] it should be mentioned that the Ashkenaz of the Bible refers to a people living somewhere in the vicinity of Mount Ararat and Armenia. The name occurs in *Genesis 10:3* and *1 Chronicles 1:6*, as one of the sons of Gomer, who was a son of Japheth. Ashkenaz is also a brother of Togarmah and a nephew of Magog whom the Khazars, according to King Joseph, claimed as their ancestor."

We get the final nail in the coffin of this 'Jewish' identity theft from Texe Marrs' website www.texemarrs.com and stunning book, *DNA Science and the Jewish Bloodline*, about the DNA of the so-called Jews. New DNA testing shows conclusively that the history which Koestler and others revealed, namely that the Ashkenazi Jews are Khazars, is now confirmed by the science of DNA.

Texe writes that the identity of the Jews was fairly well

ignored but that it began to be unravelled beginning in 1968:

> "...when the two British scientists, Watson and Crick, came up with DNA science. Since 1968, DNA has become the principal science used in criminology, both to convict and to exonerate. It has become so popular that "DNA Kits" can be purchased for a couple hundred dollars so individuals can have their own blood tested to determine their heritage, down to the last percentile. Because of DNA science, historians and anthropologists have been able to find missing links and to unravel the mysteries of race and ethnology.
>
> In 2001, Dr. Ariella Oppenheim, of Hebrew University, a biologist, published the first extensive study of DNA and the origin of the Jews. Her research found that virtually all the Jews came from Khazar blood. Not only that but Oppenheim discovered that the Palestinians—the very people whom the Jews had been persecuting and ejecting from Israel's land since 1948—had more Israelite blood than did the Jews. In sum, the vast majority of the Jews were not Jews; some of the Palestinians were. Some of the Palestinians even had a DNA chromosome which established that they were "Cohens"—workers at the ancient Temple and synagogues of the Jews."

The Definitive DNA Study

Marrs went on to publish his groundbreaking book, *DNA*

Science and the Jewish Bloodline (2013). In that book he states:

> "Now comes the ultimate, definitive DNA study, by Dr. Eran Elhaik and associates at the McKusick-Nathans Institute of Genetic Medicine, Johns Hopkins University School of Medicine. Entitled, *The Missing Link of Jewish European Ancestry: Contrasting the Rhineland and the Khazarian Hypotheses*, and published by the Oxford Journal on behalf of the Society for Molecular Biology and Evolution, the study confirms Oppenheim's research and the many scholarly books.
>
> Dr. Elhaik and the prestigious Johns Hopkins University School of Medicine conclude in their report: "The Khazarian Hypothesis suggests that Eastern European Jews descended from the Khazars, an amalgam of Turkic clans that settled the Caucasus in the early centuries and converted to Judaism in the eighth century...Following the collapse of their empire, the Judeo-Khazars fled

In 2012, Dr. Eran Elhaik of Johns Hopkins Medical University used DNA science to prove most Ashkenazi Jews are genetically related to the non-semitic Khazars, not the Biblical tribe of Judah.

> to Eastern Europe. The rise of European Jewry is therefore explained by the contribution of the Judeo-Khazars."

Who Can Argue With DNA Science?

Marrs concludes:

> "So DNA science has proven that the findings of many historians and anthropologists is correct. The "Jews" of Israel are not Abraham's descendants but, instead, come from the subjects of King Bulan of Khazaria."

Well, there you go, DNA confirms what historians have known. The Ashkenazi Jews are NOT the seed of Abraham but are really converted Khazars from the "House of Togarmah." Just as the prophecy of Ezekiel so long ago predicted. Prophecy is being fulfilled to the tee.

ARE YOU GETTING THE PICTURE?

Slowly but surely, Gog/Agag is starting to assemble the cast of characters who team up with him in *Ezekiel 38* and become part of his army. First, we have Gog himself who is Agag, King of the Amelekites/Edomites who convert to Judaism in 126 BC. Then, we have the Khazars who are of the lineage of Togarmah, or as *Ezekiel 38* says, "the house of Togarmah of the NORTH quarters" who, according to *Genesis, chapter 10:2-4,* is a nephew of Magog and brother of Ashkenaz who just so happened to give his name to the Ashkenazi Jews. Are you getting the picture? We will pick up the rest of Gog's crew as we follow his trail in the next chapters.

FOUR

GOG and Capitalism

> "He is a merchant, the balances of deceit are in his hand: he loveth to oppress."
>
> —*Hosea 12:7*

This is where the Money Matrix of Gog begins to come to power. After this mass migration of Khazar Jews into eastern Europe, Koestler tells us how these Khazars became involved in the financial industry:

> "There is a striking similarity between certain privileged positions held by Khazar Jews in Hungary and in Poland in those early days. Both the Hungarian and Polish sources refer to Jews employed as mint-masters, administrators of the royal revenue, controllers of the salt monopoly, tax collectors and "money-lenders"—i.e., bankers. That is not surprising, since foreign trade and the levying of customs duties had been the Khazars principal source of income in the past."

Behind the rise of the Jewish money-power are Satanic spiritual forces; *"the Dragon gave him his power, and his seat, and great authority" (Revelation 13:2).*

Both the Ashkenazi and Sephardic Jews seem to have a special affinity to money. This "affinity," I suppose, could be traced back biblically to being the money-changers in the Temple at Jerusalem but it has culminated in modern times to control of the world's financial system.

This special affinity for "gelt" or money has led to kings and empires employing both Ashkenazi and Sephardic Jews as financial advisors. In England, towards the end of the first millennium, and before their expulsion in 1290, the so-called Diaspora Jews of Roman and pre-Roman times were the financiers and advisors to the kings. The same situation occurred in France before they were expelled in 1391. By the way, these so-called Diaspora Jews, at their expulsion from England only numbered around 2500 and France was probably about the same. (Also please note that their expulsion was not because they went to synagogue and danced the Hora instead of going to church, but because of their stranglehold on the monetary system which was wrecking the country.) These low population figures at their expulsions confirm both Polish and Hungarian historians in that they cannot account for the multitudes of Ashkenazi Jews in Eastern Europe.

Anyhow, the main point is that, through the love of money which is the root of all kinds of evil *(1 Timothy 6:10)*, Gog and his army of avaricious Gogsters have gravitated to it as no one else in history and as a result, today they control the state banks in any country that matters. The world's financial purse strings are firmly in their hands and those hands chiefly belong to the House of Rothschild. I believe the leader of the House of Rothschild is today the manifestation of Gog in the earth.

This brings us to our 5th clue to the identity of Gog: how the Dragon brought the Prince/Lord of the House of Rothschild to the financial throne of the entire world. *"And the dragon gave him his power, and his seat, and great authority" (Revelation 13:2).*

Fifth Clue—Gog Gets Control Of The World's Money

When Rothschild arrived on the scene there were already Jewish families in many cities throughout Europe firmly entrenched as money-lenders, as bankers were called in those days. In his early career Mayer Amschel Rothschild worked for them. The following shows how the House of Rothschild ended up on top of the heap. Most of the information below is taken from ***"The Rothschild Money Trust"*** by George Armstrong. My comments are in *italics*. This was written in 1940 but it brings us up to the modern era which, since that time, has seen the Rothschilds' power grow exponentially.

MAYER AMSCHEL ROTHSCHILD, I—1743-1812.

Mayer Amschel was born in 1743 and died Sept. 29, 1812. He married Gutter Schnaper in 1770. They had a large family consisting of five sons and five daughters. He was educated as a rabbi and in his early life was both a rabbi and a junk and coin dealer. He became a money lender and in that connection acted as agent for William IX, Landgrave of Hesse-Cassel.

Mayer Amschel adopted the surname ***Rothschild*** *from the* ***red shield*** *or sign he hung atop the door to his house where he conducted business. Rothschild literally means* ***RED SHIELD*** *in German. This shield included a red hexagram star that was later adopted by the Zionist movement and incorporated in the Israeli flag as a blue star. This 6-pointed star can be interpreted geometrically as 666 (see illustration on page 52). Of course, 666 is the number of the mark of the beast of Revelation, chapter 13.*

Mayer Amschel Rothschild is Red Shield.

There is much obscurity in the history of the Rothschild family, due to the fact that their operations are secret. The conclusions here presented are based principally on Jewish or pro-Jewish history. I shall quote liberally from the *Jewish Encyclopedia* because it was, as stated in its preface, "prepared by more than 400 scholars and specialists" all of whom were Jews. It was published in 1905 and re-published in 1909. While it is a partisan history, it is on the whole, accurate in its statements of fact—it at least presents the Jewish version of the facts.

The ***Jewish Encyclopedia (JE)*** states:

> "In a latter connection (as money lender) he [Rothschild] became an agent of William IX, Landgrave Hesse-Cassel, who on his father's death in 1785 had inherited the largest private

> fortune in Europe (estimated at $40,000,000) derived mainly from the hire of troops to the British government for the putting down of the revolution in the United States.... After the battle of June in 1806 the Landgrave fled to Denmark, leaving 600,000 pounds (about $3,000,000) with Mayer Rothschild for safe keeping."
>
> "According to legend this money was hidden away in wine casks and, escaping the search of Napoleon's soldiers when they entered Frankfort, was restored intact in the same casks in 1814 when the elector returned to the electorate. The facts are somewhat less romantic and more businesslike."—*JE*

The reason the *Jewish Encyclopedia* says the facts are entirely "less romantic and more businesslike," is because the encyclopedia views them from the Jewish Talmudic 'business' perspective, in which all Goyim property belongs to the Jews and to which they are entitled to take through any means they can. The Prophet Hosea sheds a little more light on these business practices: *"He is a merchant, the balances of deceit are in his hands: he loveth to oppress" (Hosea 12:7).*

They are "more businesslike" because Mayer Amschel Rothschild embezzled the money. This money was tainted from its very origin. It was paid by the British government to the Landgrave for the services of his soldiers, used to suppress the American revolution, and the soldiers were morally entitled to it. It was first embezzled by William of Hesse and then by Mayer Amschel.

This twice-stolen money is the foundation of the huge Rothschild fortune. It has ever since been true to its origin.

Six outside triangles. Six sides on the inside of the star. Six sides on the two large triangles=666. Plus it is the number of a man, the mark on the shield of Rothschild.

There is not an honestly acquired dollar in the hundreds of billions now possessed by the Rothschild family.

Instead of putting the money in wine casks, Mayer Rothschild sent the entire sum with his son Nathan, to London, and so established the London branch of the family.

> "Nathan invested it in large sums of gold from the East India Company, knowing that it would be needed for Wellington's peninsula campaign [against Napoleon in 1815]. Through this he made no less than four profits: (1) on the sale of Wellington's paper (which he bought at 50c on the dollar and collected at par); (2) on the sale of gold to Wellington; (3) on its re-purchase; and (4) on forwarding it to Portugal. This was the beginning of the great fortune." *JE p. 494*

Well, there was actually a little more to the story than the *Jewish Encyclopedia* tells us. They left out the part about Nathan's manipulation of the London stock market through deception. In fact, the bulk of the fortune made off of the Wellington investment was NOT made off of that investment it was made because Nathan manipulated the London stock market through deceit. It is this deception that is the hallmark of the Rothschild way of 'investing.' They make money the old-fashioned way, they steal it. And here is how Nathan pulled it off: Nathan had positioned himself and his agents on French and Belgium soil near the battle line. His agent saw Napoleon's defeat at the hands of Wellington's army and sent Nathan, who was near Paris, word of the defeat by carrier pigeon.

The historian John Reeves, in his book, *"The Rothschilds,"* describes vividly how upon Nathan's return from near the battle of Waterloo, he went posthaste to the English Channel and there hired a boat at excessive cost and crossed the English channel in stormy weather, and from there rushed to the London stock exchange, appearing muddy and dejected, where he passed out the word that Wellington had been defeated at Waterloo, and reinforced this by ostentatiously dumping stocks on the market. This created a great panic upon the exchange and everybody dumped their stocks at sacrifice prices. In the meantime Nathan, through his agents, was secretly buying them.

They still 'gamble' on world events like this, only today they control so much that the outcome is pretty well determined beforehand.

There were no telegraphs or telephones or radios or fast posts in those days. It was several days before the news reached London that Wellington had won the battle of Waterloo. There was then great rejoicing and the stock market rebounded and stocks went to unprecedented heights, when Nathan unloaded his stocks.

This is precisely the method that the Rothschilds have followed since, and is one of the methods by which they have amassed their huge fortune.

This was indeed much "less romantic and more businesslike." With this vast sum of money, branches of the

House of Rothschild were established in Berlin, Paris, Vienna and Naples, with one of the brothers in charge of each of them. All of these houses were exceedingly prosperous, particularly the London and Paris branches.

> "Nathan boasted that he had multiplied their capital 2500 times in the course of five years" *(The Rothschilds, Financial Rulers of Nations, p. 167).*

If this is true, it means that at that time *[about 1820]* the capital of the English branch had been increased from $3,000,000 to about $7,500,000,000.

The Jew, Benjamin Disraeli, *[later Prime Minister of Great Britain]* in his novel, *"Coningsby,"* names Nathan and also his son, Lionel, as "Sidonia." He says of the elder "Sidonia."

> "He arrived here *[London]* after the peace of Paris with his large capital. He staked all that he was worth on the Waterloo loan *[to the British government for Wellington's army]* and the event made him one of the greatest capitalists in Europe.... He reaped the due reward of his sagacity [and deceit]. Europe did require money and Sidonia was ready to lend it to Europe. France wanted some, Austria more, Prussia a little, Russia a few millions; Sidonia could furnish them all."

Disraeli says of him further:

> "He established a brother or a near relative in

> whom he could confide, in most of the principal capitals. He was lord and master of the money markets of the world and of course virtually lord and master of everything else. He literally held the revenues of southern Italy in pawn, and monarchs and ministers of all countries courted his advice and were guided by his suggestions."

It was probably Mayer Amschel's purpose in the beginning to establish a *Jewish dynasty* with his male descendants as rulers. Whether that was his purpose or not, it was the *effect* of his will. He established the kingdom of the Jews that has since been governed by his male descendants. *[Word is that it is now governed by a cabal of international bankers who vote on decisions to be made with Rothschild being the final deciding vote with his yay or nay; Rothschild's vote can only be overridden with a ¾ majority vote.]*

We cannot know whether at that time he had in contemplation a Jewish world empire. Apparently this was a later development. There is good reason to believe that this ambitious enterprise was initiated by Theodore Herzl. Herzl was an active, ambitious, Jewish rabbi-politician and an intense hater of the Gentiles. He was given credit for organizing modern Zionism at a conference of leaders in Basle, Switzerland, in 1897. It is thought that at that meeting some of the Protocols were adopted as precepts for the establishment of the contemplated Jewish empire.

Herzl probably organized two important Jewish organizations: (1) a secret super-organization to be composed of 300 men whose identity should be kept secret and who would constitute the super-government for the Jewish race; (2) a popular religious organization to be composed of 450 delegates selected by the rabbis and the Hebrew churches.

Through Herzl's activities, the Secret Committee of 300 was established for the management of the political power of the huge estate with the consent of the Rothschilds. It is known that Theodore Herzl was an intimate personal friend of Lord Rothschild II.

Mayer Amschel Rothschild I, was succeeded upon his death by his third son, Nathan, of London. Nathan had uncanny and unscrupulous financial ability. He had, prior to Amschel's death, established the private banking house of N. M. Rothschild & Sons, and added enormously to the family fortune. It appears that the elder brother, Mayer Amschel, Jr., who continued in charge of the Frankfort branch, recognized the superior qualifications of Nathan and was willing to waive his right by virtue of *primo geniture*. Nathan was therefore chosen by the four brothers as his father's successor.

NATHAN ROTHSCHILD

Nathan married the sister-in-law of Moses Montefiore, thus coming into association with the heads of the **Sephardic** community then ruling the financial world of London through their connection with Amsterdam *(Jewish Encyclopedia, Vol. X, p. 494)*.

Nathan is described by the historian John Reeves, a Rothschild partisan, as being a very shrewd, unscrupulous and uncouth man, and exceedingly closefisted. He says that, "he never paid his employees a farthing more than was necessary for their bare subsistence or at least not a farthing more than they could compel him to pay" *(The Rothschilds—Financial Rulers of Nations)*.

Reeves, adds another glimpse into the Rothschild business practice:

"One cause of his (Nathan's) success was the

secrecy with which he shrouded, and the tortuous policy with which he misled those who watched him the keenest" (p. 189).

Nathan, the 2nd Red Rothschild.

And this principle, it may be added, has governed the management of the Rothschild fortune from its beginning to this hour.

Nathan established the private banking firm of N. M. Rothschild & Sons in London, with branches in Paris, Berlin, Vienna and Naples. This firm operates on the exchanges, underwrites government and other loans; it is the agent and manager of banks, railways, steel, munitions, and other corporations. It has branches under many names. In America it is represented by Kuhn, Loeb & Co., and formerly by August Belmont & Co. It is probable also that J. P. Morgan & Co., Seligman & Co., Speyer & Co., Lehman & Co., and other private Jewish banks are its undercover branches.

What we are witnessing today is the complete takeover of every nation by the Rothschilds and their USA Federal Reserve Bank, City of London, European Central Bank, the IMF, World Bank, and Bank of International Settlements—THIS WILL LEAD TO WW3 AND THEIR HOPED FOR NEW WORLD ORDER.

Lionel Rothschild, the eldest son of Nathan, succeeded him as the head and managing partner of N. M. Rothschild & Sons. At his death in 1879, Lionel's eldest son, Nathan Mayer (Lord Rothschild 1st) succeeded him. The *Jewish Encyclopedia* states that:

> "In 1885 he (Nathan) was raised to the peerage and was the first Jew to take his seat in the House of Lords, an event which was regarded as completing the emancipation of the Jews… Lord Rothschild is a governor of the Bank of England and a presiding officer of many great corporations… In 1902 he was appointed a member of the Royal Commission on Alien Immigration, an office that brought him in touch with the late Theodore Herzl."

This was the beginning of the transformation of the British House of Lords from a Gentile landed aristocracy to a Jewish plutocracy, and of the government from a Gentile to a Jewish government. It is reported that there are now [In 1940] sixty Jews in the House of Lords without counting the hybrids that should in fact be included. They are today thoroughly interbred with the 'Royals' of Britain.

As a Rabbi, schooled in the racist teachings of the Talmud, Mayer Amschel Rothschild hated the Gentiles with an intense religious hatred and that hatred has been handed down from generation to generation. It is hatred that demands vengeance upon the Gentile race—"an eye for an eye and a tooth for a tooth." It is shown in every paragraph, every sentence and every word in the three codes of the family, viz., the Talmud, the protocols, and the code of the communists.

Nathan Mayer Rothschild died in 1915 and was succeeded by his eldest son, Lionel Walter, the second Lord Rothschild, as the head of the banking firm N. M. Rothschild & Sons. He appears to have been a member of the Council of the Jewish Agency. He died in 1937 and was succeeded as head of the

Warren Buffett, Arnold Schwarzenegger, and Lord Jacob Rothschild at Waddesdon Manor, Rothschild's estate in England. This was the summer of 2002, just prior to Arnie making his bid for Governor. California is the 10th largest economy in the world and Rothschild wanted to make sure Arnie would be a good manager. Looks like he thought Schwarzenegger was the guy for the job.

London branch of the banking firm by his eldest son, Nathan Mayer Victor (third Lord Rothschild).

Today, Lord Jacob Rothschild is running the show. See his photo here with Arnold Schwarzenegger and Warren Buffet.

To get an idea of just how vast the Rothschild fortune is, we go back to the boast of Nathan Rothschild who said he increased the family fortune from $3,000,000 to about $7,500,000,000 within five years time, which would be in about 1820.

That would mean an increase of 500% a year, but that was, based on a huge gamble of staking all he had on Wellingtons victory and the manipulation of the London stock market so it's not likely that this rate of increase continued. But it is probable that he continued to increase it at the rate of 10% or more, annually. At this rate it would have amounted to approximately 20,000,000,000 by 1840.

If you are used to today's banksters talking in trillions of dollars, 20 billion doesn't sound like a lot, but most of today's 'money' is just super inflated paper and computer entries. However, in the 1840s all the paper money was pretty much anchored to gold or silver and was actually worth something. For instance, in the 1920s you could buy an ounce of gold for $20 dollars—today it's around $1200 dollars and will probably go through the roof. Or rather it will go as high as the Rothschilds want it to go since they set the price of it everyday from their headquarters in the City of London.

We can take pencil and paper and figure accurately the increase of $20,000,000,000 at 5% compound interest in 100 years time, but it is impossible to even approximate the profits from thc manipulation of the exchanges.

By virtue of their immense financial power they have been able to raise or lower prices at will, to create a boom or bring on a depression, to buy when stocks and commodities are cheap, and to sell when they are high.

It was stated by the Russian Major General, Count Cherep-Spiridovich, that the Rothschild family fortune in 1925 was $300,000,000,000, and that they made $100,000,000,000 of that sum out of the late world war, now called World War I. *(The Secret World Government or "The Hidden Hand").*

It is likely that the Rothschild family fortune was, in 1940, in the neighborhood of $500,000,000,000, which was about twice the value of the wealth of all the people of the United States.

There are many other rich Jews in addition to the Rothschilds, but the huge Rothschild fortune represents the greater part of the wealth of all the Jews of the world. The

Our family owns Bank of America, Goldman Sachs, the Federal Reserve Bank, the World Bank, the IMF, the Bank of International Settlements, the Global Environment Facility (The Climate Change Bank) and ALL the money in your pocket. We create money out of thin air and make you buy it with interest! We are the Hammer that is bent on crushing to pieces the last vestiges of your culture. We are the Sickle that will reap all your labor and all your wealth. You are living in our Money Matrix. We lead the Army of Ezekiel 38. We are GOG!

authority mentioned says:

> "The Rothschilds were not without competitors; other Jewish families, the Lazards, Sterns, Speyers, and Seligmans adopted the Rothschild plan" *(Jewish Encyclopedia. Vol. 2, p. 496)*.

The Rothschilds, through the Sassoons (one of the female branches of their family), own and control the banks of China and India. They also own, control and operate the immensely profitable, illicit opium trade.

A number of rich Catholics undertook to organize a competitor bank to rival the Rothschild power. I have been unable to discover when this enterprise was launched, but it was sometime about 1830. The Rothschilds crushed it. The *Jewish Encyclopedia* admits that:

> "The failure of the Catholic bank left the Rothschilds still more absolutely the undisputed

leaders of French finance, but left also a legacy of hatred which had much influence on the growth of the anti-Semitic movement in France" *(Jewish Encyclopedia. Vol. 2, p. 497).*

It says further:

"It is a somewhat curious sequel to the attempt to set up a Catholic competitor to the Rothschilds that at the present time (1905) the latter are the guardians of the papal treasure" *(Jewish Encyclopedia. Vol. 2, p. 497).*

If this latter statement is true, the Rothschilds' control in addition to their own fortune, the immense liquid resource of the Catholic Church, which is second only to the Rothschilds in wealth and power. It is probably not literally true since the private banking firm did not do commercial banking. It is likely that the papal treasure is deposited with the Bank of England or some other bank "front," but even so it contributes to the Rothschild power.

The Catholics, with their Jesuits, have their own conspiracy going on; but without the control of world finance in their hands, they, too, are subservient to the Rothschilds as can be seen in the last two popes putting their blessing on Zionism.

It should be observed from the above quotation that the Rothschilds brought on a major depression *[In order to crush the Catholic bank in France]* which provoked anti-Semitism. I identify this as the catastrophe of 1839-1840, known as the "hungry forties," which our American historians have wrongfully ascribed to the veto of the charter of the Second Bank of the United States by Andrew Jackson in 1836.

The next major depression in this country and throughout

the world was in 1873—"the crime of '73." This was brought about by the demonetization of silver. The Rothschilds had already brought about the demonetization of silver in Germany as a part of their plan to "facilitate the payment of the French indemnity to Germany," but it was necessary to the perfection of this plan that the gold standard be established in America. Through bribery, they caused to be clandestinely inserted a clause in the Coinage Act of 1873 that demonetized silver.

The next major depression in America and throughout the world was the **panic of 1893**, which was brought about by the competition between the Jewish House of Rothschild and the Jewish rival firm of Baring Brothers. The ruler of the Rothschilds determined to crush the Baring firm. The *Jewish Encyclopedia* says of this operation:

> "Similarly it is stated that the financial crisis of Germany and Austria [and America and the world] was also a source of anti-Semitism because the shrewdness of the Jewish bankers had foreseen the crash and they were enabled to evade it" *(Jewish Encyclopedia Vol. 2, p. 493)*.

The Jewish banksters are always able to **'foresee'** and **'evade'** these **depressions** because they create them. They not only evade these crises but they sell their securities in advance of them and buy them back when values have been destroyed, at a fraction of their former worth, and thereby make immense profits. It is by the repetition of this process from panic to panic that they have so rapidly acquired the wealth of the world. The Jews do not lose on a panic, for the word is passed down when it is to happen. They usually profit by it; a panic is their rich harvest.

The next major panic was that of 1907 which the Rothschild

controlled banks created by refusing to pay their customers and their bank correspondents the money due them and which was held on deposit. They simply coldly and brutally said to the other bankers having deposits with them: 'We cannot and will not pay you your money, and you must take care of your own customers the best way you can.' This resulted in all the banks throughout the country clamping down on their customers and refusing to pay them their money, which in turn resulted in checking all commercial enterprises and a great fall in the wage and price level and a disastrous panic.

It resulted also in the people and the bankers getting together for the purpose of organizing a currency and credit expanding system to prevent a recurrence of such a panic. And worst of all, the outcome was that the Rothschilds organized this system for us and created one that they could manipulate in bringing about future panics and through which they could fix and regulate the wage and price level. That system has been responsible for the depressions of 1920, 1930 and the Roosevelt depression of 1937 which resulted in the "New Deal" and general bankruptcy.

Of course, that system is the Federal Reserve, which is as 'federal' as Federal Express. It is in fact a private bank whose controlling members are the international banksters headed by Rothschild. Whenever the Rothschilds decide it, the world finds itself in a Greater Depression engineered by Rothschild banksters in which they intend to bring about a 'controlled chaos' that will leave them firmly enthroned as the absolute despotic rulers of this world—believe it or not.

We have had these depressions so frequently and regularly that we have come to regard them as natural phenomena. There are economists who attempted to predict them. They usually occur about every ten years. They have all been manipulated, and for the same purpose, viz., thievery and robbery and to establish the Kingdom of Judah throughout the world.

As cruel and destructive as these panics are, they are not as bad as war. The Rothschild power was responsible for World War I and for the very destructive world war *[WW2]*. They have been responsible for most of the wars that have occurred within the last 150 years. They usually finance both sides of these wars, not because they are interested in either side winning but because wars are demoralizing and destructive to the Gentiles and because they bring the Jews nearer their ultimate goal, viz., rulers of the world.

Wars are their shortest and quickest route to the throne. The accumulation of compound interest is entirely too slow for them. The robbery of the people through their manipulation of money and credit, as effective as it is, is also too slow. War, with all of its attendant human misery, is their surest and best route—and so we have wars and will continue to have them so long as this power dominates the world.

In his 1844 novel, *Coningsby*, Disraeli has "Sidonia" (Rothschild) saying the following eye-opening statement about Jewish control of world finance:

> "I had on my arrival (at St. Petersburg) an interview with the Russian Minister of Finance, Count Cancrin; I beheld the son of a Lithuanian Jew… I had an audience on my arrival at Madrid with the Spanish minister; I beheld one like myself, the son of a Nuovo Christiano, a Jew of Aragon. In consequence of what transpired at Madrid I went straight to consult the President of the French Council; I beheld the son of a French Jew… We fixed on Prussia… Count Arnim entered the cabinet, and I beheld a Prussian Jew.

> So you see, my dear Coningsby, that the world is governed by very different personages to what is imagined by those who are not behind the scenes"
> *"Coningsby"* by Benjamin Disraeli, p. 207-209.

****

This brings us to the end of Armstrong's history of the Rothschilds. We could go on, and on, and on, but the point I want to anchor your mind on is the power of Edomite-Jewish Money, particularly as it is manifested in the House of Rothschild—for they are the modern manifestation of Gog/Agag, the King of the Jews and King of the Money of the World and hoping soon to be King Despot of the World.

Up to the time of the early part of the 1900s, the control of GOG/Jewish power was mainly the power of and the attraction of money. They reigned over the Gentile nations much like a whore has 'control' over a sex-crazed, drunken sailor thru the 'charms' of her sexual attraction, which is to say, very tenuous at best. But this is the way Jesus himself described Gog's 'power' in the Book of Revelation—as a whore sitting on a beast! Did you know that the Talmud says in several places that the Gentiles are beasts?

The Talmud says Goy/Gentiles differ only in form from beasts, in other words, Gentiles are merely beasts in human form. In *Midrasch Talpioth (fol. 225d)* it says:

> "God created them in the form of men for the glory of Israel...Akum (Gentiles) were created for the sole end of ministering unto them [the Jews] day and night. Nor can they ever be relieved from this service. It is becoming to the son of a king [an Israelite] that animals in their natural form, and animals in the form of human

beings should minister unto him."

With such racist teaching crammed into his brain, no wonder former Israeli Prime Minister, Menachem Begin, is quoted as saying "Palestinians are beasts on two legs." Zionist sites have said this was never said by Begin—but why not? He would only be quoting from the Talmud!

But maybe the Talmud is right, because most Gentile Christians support the Israelis whose official religious book says Jesus Christ is in hell in boiling fecal matter. Maybe they are beasts! It is similar to the way the Lord reveals the picture in the Book of Revelation. There He gives a vivid picture of a drunken Babylon/Talmud/Whore riding atop her Gentile/Beast (Just like our illustration of 'Christian' Zionists in chapter 6).

"And on her forehead was a name written, Babylon the Great mother of harlots and abominations of the earth" (Revelation 17:5). The ONLY religion that has a Babylonian book as the basis of their religion and culture is the one that has the Babylonian Talmud. Babylon is "written" on their foreheads—On their minds. But sometimes when you look at how this little 'sexual/money' tryst is played out in real time it's hard to distinguish who is the whore and who is the beast as they have become one flesh! This Whore is "dressed in scarlet and…rides upon a scarlet colored Beast." Edom means Red, Rothschild means Red Shield, the Commies are Red—They are all one! *(And we can't forget all those scarlet robed Cardinals from whence came Jesuit Father Jorge Mario BerGOGlia who recently became Pope Francis, another GOGster in disguise?)*

In the early part of the last century things began looking up for Gog a lot! This is when Gog moved from just being the money-whore for the kings of the earth into absolute dictatorial control over nations. The Babylon money whore began to *"rule over the kings of the earth" (Revelation 17:18).*

Now while the modern nation of "Israel" was founded in 1948, its coming was first signalled by the Balfour Declaration in 1917. The takeover of the U.S.S.R. in 1917 was further confirmation that Gog was on the move toward his final goal.

This brings us to the 6th clue to the identity of Gog.

FIVE

GOG and Communism

SIXTH CLUE—Gog becomes Prince of Rosh/ Russia and attacks the "mountains of Israel."

Two events took place in one week of November 1917, that began to take Gog to an entirely new level—Gog began the actual **physical**, war against the "mountains of Israel!" This is where our trail of clues leads us to and where I believe the prophecy in the Book of Ezekiel, Chapter 38 commences, it begins in one week of November, 1917.

1—On November 2nd, 1917, Britain issued the so-called *Balfour Declaration* giving the Jews the country of Palestine. This 'Declaration' of British support, which is printed later in the chapter, is addressed to **Lord Rothschild!**

2—On November 7th, 1917, the Rothschild-financed, Jewish-led Bolshevik Communists took over Russia and "Gog" became the "Prince of Rosh/Russia, Meshech/Moscow and Tubal/Tolbolsk."

I believe that this week in 1917 begins the prophecy of *Ezekiel 38* and *39*. It begins with the British "Balfour Declaration" which launched the official Zionist/Gog invasion of the literal/physical "LAND of Israel." Communist/Gog

Lenin's grandfather was Israel Blank, a Jew. This is now confirmed by Soviet records.

Karl Marx, father of Communism, was Jewish and from a long line of Rabbis. Marx wrote the manual of communism, *Das Kapital*. It was a book all about money but without one mention of his Rothschild cousin who controlled most of it. Jacob Schiff, of Rothschild-owned Kuhn Loeb & Co. banking, gave $20 million in gold to Lenin and Trotsky to finance the Communist revolution in 1917. Schiff was only one of many Jewish financiers who bankrolled Communism, their supposed enemy. Why? Their idea was to create and control two 'opposing' forces with which they hope to bring about a final synthesis. That synthesis is their New World Order with them at the helm and in total control of every thing on the planet; a totally insane, megalomaniacal, dream which has become the world's nightmare.

physically conquered his first spiritual *"MOUNTAIN of Israel" (Ezekiel 38:8)*, the 'officially' Orthodox Christian nation of Russia, and "Gog" became the "Prince of Rosh" the literal physical dictator of Russia.

This prophecy is both a physical manifestation of Gog's conquest of Palestine and a symbolic manifestation of Gog's conquest of spiritual Israel, the Christianized nations of the world.

"Mountains" in scripture always symbolize "kingdoms." The Kingdom of Babylon is called a *"destroying Mountain"* in *Jeremiah, chapter 51:25*. Isaiah said the *"Mountain of the Lords house shall be exalted above the mountains" (Isaiah 2:2)*. In other words, the Kingdom of the Lord will eventually reign over all other kingdoms. And Daniel said *"the Mountain of the Lord shall fill all the earth and his kingdom shall stand forever" (Daniel 2:34, 44)*.

The next chapter goes into more detail on this topic of what really constitutes 'Israel.' Let's just say that in the New Testament, Paul the Apostle defines the "Israel of God" as those who are believers in Jesus Christ *(Galatians 6:15,16)*. The land that was given to Israel (Not Khazars, Edomites, or disinherited Judah/Jews) is actually there in the Middle East, but that land was always just to be symbolic of the real 'land' which is our own biological bodies, made from the "dust of the ground" which now belong to Jesus Christ our King. Christians, collectively, are the very "Temple" of God.

Jesus is the "King of Israel." When we become Christians, we acknowledge Jesus' kingship over us and we become Israel. *"The Israel of God"* physically occupies countries that this "Israel" lives in, which, until recently, was mainly in the West. China today probably has more real Christians than the West, South Korea is not far behind either, not to mention Africa. However, most of these nations never became an 'official' Christian nation like the nations of Europe, the Americas, Australia, New Zealand, etc. These nations became the nations that Gog is invading and conquering at the same time as they are conquering the 'symbolic' land of Israel in the Middle East.

Russia was an official Christian Orthodox nation. It was the first "mountain of Israel" that Gog became Prince over; the United States will be the last. Then Gog will have total physical control of the planet. What will happen then? More than likely: *"Great Tribulation such as was not since the beginning of the age no nor ever shall be"—Jesus Christ (Matthew 24:15-21).*

You ask, "How can God let this happen?" It happens because of the corruption of these so-called Christian nations which were really only 'Christian' in name. Gog's Antichrist takeover of the world is a judgement of God. Get it? What makes it so interesting is that it is all laid out in this ancient prophecy of Ezekiel.

Here's how Gog invaded and took military and political control of the first Christian "Mountain of Israel," which was

Is the USA having a déjà vu of the USSR? The Jew Lenin and the Jew Chertoff.

Russia. Remember, Gog is in Jewry and is the King of the Jews.

It is a well-known fact that the Commie Jewish/Bolsheviks were financed by Jewish interests in the West. Only a few months prior to the communist takeover in November, at a Bolshevik rally in New York's Carnegie Hall on the night of 23 March 1917, a telegram of support from the Jew, Jacob Schiff of Kuhn, Loeb & Co. (Rothschild bankers in the United States), was read out loud. *The Telegram* was reprinted in the next morning's *The New York Times*. Schiff later tried to deny his involvement, but thirty years later his grandson John admitted in *The New York Journal-American* (3 February 1949) that the old man had sunk twenty million dollars into the Bolshevik cause. [$20,000,000 in 1917 dollars translates to about $212,245,000 in today's inflated money). And Shiff was only one of many Jews that contributed to the 'cause.'

Another Western banker who poured funds into Bolshevik Russia was the Jew, Olaf Ashberg, of the Stockholm Nia Banken, another Rothschild bank. He remained the Soviets' paymaster until the late 1940s. *The London Evening Standard* of 6 September 1948 reported a visit by Ashberg to Switzerland "for secret meetings with Swiss government officials and banking executives." Diplomatic circles describe Mr. Ashberg as the 'Soviet banker' who advanced large sums to Lenin and Trotsky in 1917. At the time of the revolution, Mr. Ashberg gave Trotsky money to form and equip the first unit of the Red Army.

The Bolsheviks also received assistance from the Al Gore family's old buddy, the late Jewish financier, Armand Hammer, who before his death, commuted back and forth between New York and Moscow to take care of his business interests in both communities. Hammer's *Occidental Oil Company* built a 1600 mile chemical pipeline in southern Russia. He was also on such good terms with the Soviets that he personally arranged for Soviet art galleries to lend paintings to America. Hammer's father, Julius, was one of the *founders* of the communist party in the United States.

Several historians have shown that financial and industrial interests in the West are largely responsible for building the industrial infrastructure of their supposed enemies, the Soviet Union. This vast build up of the Soviet Union is minutely detailed in Antony Sutton's eye-opening book, *The Best Enemy Money Can Buy,* (Liberty House Press 1-800-343-6180). Sutton shows how US finance and technology given to the USSR is responsible for most of the industrial infrastructure of the Soviet Union built during the so-called 'Cold War'—so much so in fact that some have said Russian products should have carried the label, "Made in the USA." While Sutton quipped, "We have the best enemies that our money can buy." Almost all of this American 'help' to the then cold-war enemies of the USA was funneled through the Jewish–controlled US State Department.

An American Senate subcommittee investigation into the Russian Revolution heard evidence, put on congressional record, that "(I)n December 1919, under the presidency of a man named Apelbaum (Zinovieff)... out of the 388 members of the Bolshevik central government, only 16 happened to be real Russians, and all the rest (with the exception of a Negro from the U.S.) were Jews" (U.S. Senate Document 62, 1919).

Of the 25 leaders of the Bolshevik communist revolution, all of them were Jews, even Lenin! Lenin's maternal grandfather, Israel Blank, was a Jew. Lenin was aware of his 'Jewish' roots and once wrote, "The best revolutionaries are Jews"—undoubtedly referring to himself. Under Israel's "Law of Return," Jewishness is counted from the mothers side. But since Lenin's mother's Jewishness could not be transmitted

Pictured here is the respected Chief Rabbi of the United States during the 1930s, Stephen S. Wise. When asked what he thought about communism he replied, "Some call it Marxism, but I call it Judaism" (*The American Bulletin*, May 5, 1935). Just mull those words over for a little bit and maybe your brain will kick into gear.

from her father, then Lenin wouldn't have been considered a full-blown Jew, if he were alive today. That means he wouldn't have been able to make 'Aliyah' or 'Return' to 'Israel' as a "Jew"—too bad huh?—but maybe his wife could have got him in since she was a Jew.

The overwhelming Jewishness of communism led Stephen Wise, the chief rabbi of the United States in the 1930s, to declare, "Some call it Marxism, but I call it Judaism."

But what about Stalin, he was a Russian wasn't he? Well, according to Jewish sources he was a Jew. The Jewish writer, Louis Levine, in *Soviet Russia Today* (Nov. 1946), wrote: "Stalin and the father of his Jewish son-in-law drank 'Lachaim'

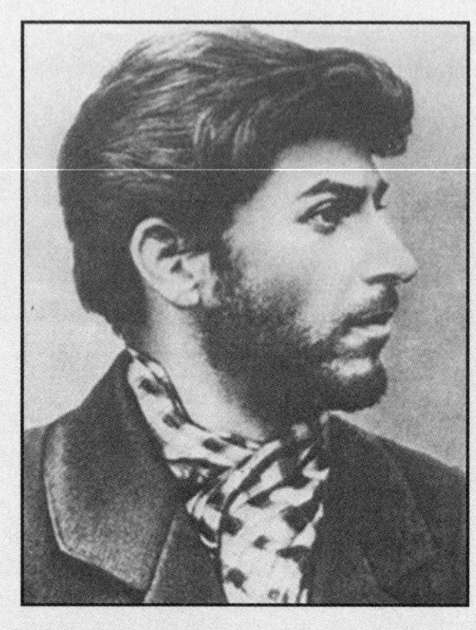

Here's a picture of a young Stalin. He spoke Yiddish. Jewish publications in 1946 and 1950 said Stalin was Jewish. Why revise their statements now? His 'anti-semitism' was just Zionist gang wars and Stalin lost.

together in the Kremlin." Again, David Weissman, in an article in *The B'nai B'rith Messenger* (March 3, 1950), says that Stalin is a Jew. This quote is also in *Judaism and Bolshevism* (The Britons Publishing Society). What happened under Stalin was a war between rival Jewish gangs, just like the Mafia gangs. Stalin eventually lost and the winning gang spun the whole thing off with the fiction that Stalin was an anti-semite, so the Jews could maintain their 'victim' status.

You have to remember that deception is the main game in town and these guys are getting spiritual help and their game plan from the "Father of lies" Satan himself. This is the great deception Jesus warned would happen just before His Return and which Paul said would be a deception sent from God Himself because they would not believe the truth. *"Because they received not the love of the truth, for this cause God shall send them strong delusion that they should believe a lie" (2 Thessalonians 2:12).* If you consider yourself a "Christian-Zionist or Judeo-Christian" you are believing a LIE! Actually it's lies, upon lies, upon lies.

The following are the names of the Jewish leaders of the Russian revolution as appears from the *American Official Services Report, Section III:*

Assumed Name	Real Name	Nationality
Lenin	Oulianow (Ulianoff)	Part-Jewish
Trotsky (Trotzky)	Bronstein	Jewish
Steckloff	Nakhames	Jewish
Martoff	Zederbaum	Jewish
Zinovieff	Apfelbaum	Jewish
Kameneff	Rosenfeld	Jewish
Dan Gourevitch	(Yurewitsch)	Jewish
Ganetzky	Furstenberg	Jewish
Parvus	Helpfand	Jewish
Uritzky	Padomilsky	Jewish
Larin	Lurge	Jewish
Bohrin	Nathansohn	Jewish
Martinoff	Zibar	Jewish
Bogdanoff	Zilberstein	Jewish
Garin	Garfeld	Jewish
Suchanoff	Gimel	Jewish
Kairmelff	Goldmann	Jewish

Churchill wrote about the Jewish-led communist takeover of Russia in the Feburary 8, 1920 issue of the *Illustrated Sunday Herald of London.*

> *"There is no need to exaggerate the part played in the **creation of Bolshevism** and in the actual bringing about of the **Russian Revolution** by these international and for the most part atheistical Jews. It is certainly a very great one; it probably outweighs all others. With the notable*

exception of Lenin, the majority of the leading figures are Jews. Moreover, the principal inspiration and driving power comes from the Jewish leaders. Thus, Tchitcherin, a pure Russian, is eclipsed by his nominal subordinate Litvinoff, and the influence of Russians like Bukharin or Lunacharski cannot be compared with the power of Trotsky, or of Zinovieff, the Dictator of the Red Citadel (Petrograd), or of Krasin or Radek—all Jews.

"In the Soviet institutions the predominance of Jews is even more astonishing. And the prominent, if not indeed the principal, part in the system of terrorism applied by the Extraordinary Commissions for Combating Counter-Revolution has been taken by Jews, and in some notable cases by Jewesses."

However, in this very same article, Churchill gives his solution to the Jewish/communist problem, by telling the Jews that instead of getting involved in communism they should hook-up with the Zionist led invasion of Palestine under British protection to establish a Jewish state.

"Zionism offers the ***third sphere*** *to the political conceptions of the Jewish race. In violent contrast to international communism, it presents to the Jew a national idea of a commanding character. It has fallen to the British Government, as the result of the conquest of Palestine, to have the opportunity and the responsibility of securing for the Jewish race all over the world a home and a*

centre of national life. The statesmanship and historic sense of Mr. Balfour were prompt to seize this opportunity. Declarations have been made which have irrevocably decided the policy of Great Britain. The fiery energies of Dr. Weissman, the leader, for practical purposes, of the Zionist project, backed by many of the most prominent British Jews, and supported by the full authority of Lord Allenby, are all directed to achieving the success of this inspiring movement.

"The struggle which is now beginning between the Zionist and Bolshevik Jews is little less than a struggle for the soul of the Jewish people."

The reality is that **Zionism, Communism** and **Capitalism** are the three-legged stool on which sits Gog/Rothschild, King of the Jews. For it is Rothschild money and banking interests that control and finance all three.

Now we will look at how Gog began his invasion of the 'mountains of Israel' in Palestine.

The British Foreign Secretary, Lord Arthur James Balfour, a Jew, is credited with drafting the letter which is commonly known as the "Balfour Declaration," which is reprinted below.

Foreign Office
November 2nd, 1917

Dear Lord Rothschild,

I have much pleasure in conveying to you, on behalf of His Majesty's Government, the following declaration of sympathy with Jewish Zionist aspirations which has been submitted to, and approved by, the Cabinet.

His Majesty's Government view with favour the establishment in Palestine of a national home for the Jewish people, and will use their best endeavours to facilitate the achievement of this object, it being clearly understood that nothing shall be done which may prejudice the civil and religious rights of existing non-Jewish communities in Palestine, or the rights and political status enjoyed by Jews in any other country.

I should be grateful if you would bring this declaration to the knowledge of the Zionist Federation.

Yours sincerely,
Arthur James Balfour

Notice to whom the letter is addressed: ***"Dear Lord Rothschild."*** That would be Lord Lionel Rothschild. Five weeks after the *Balfour Declaration*, the Turks surrendered Jerusalem to British forces, virtually without a fight. The Foreign Office appointed a Jew, Sir Herbert Samuel, as British High Commissioner of Palestine. Abba Eban (former Prime Minister of Israel) called the Balfour Declaration, which opened the way for the creation of Israel, *"the authentic turning point in Jewish political history."*

The British mandate over Palestine was finally approved on July 24, 1922, and officially endorsed by ten nations

[Serbia, France, Italy, Greece, Holland, Siam, China, Japan, United States and England]. The terms of the mandate imposed on Britain the obligation to secure the establishment of the Jewish national home, to facilitate Jewish immigration and to encourage Jewish settlements on the land.

What becomes apparent in all of this is that without the subservient docile help of the Gentile 'beast,' none of this could have happened. In fact, the Gentile 'beast' is the one that carried the Jewish whore in the Book of Revelation to power! These Gentile powers are really what the Talmud and the Book of Revelation calls them: "Beasts in human form."

All 'Christian' Zionists are just like their Jewish masters say they are: *"God created them [Gentiles] in the form of men for the glory of Israel. But Akum [Gentiles] were created for the sole end of ministering unto them [the Jews] day and night. Nor can they ever be relieved from this service. It is becoming to the son of a king [an Israelite] that animals in their natural form, and animals in the form of human beings should minister unto him" (Midrasch Talpioth, fol. 225d, Talmud).*

The fact that the Jews are a mixed bag of Edomites and Khazars, the "house of Togarmah" etc, is an historical reality. I believe they also include original Judaic blood as well. The only reason to deny the latter, is because you subscribe to such equally racist and unbiblical beliefs as the Talmud. According to Jesus Himself the original Judaics who rejected Him were rejected and cut off by God: *"The Kingdom shall be taken away from you and given to a nation bringing forth the fruits thereof" (Matthew 21).* In other words, God couldn't "take it away" from them unless they first had it. They did have the kingdom and God took it away. Now the only true Jews and true Israel today are those who have faith in the King of the Jews, Jesus Christ, who inherited the Throne of David over Israel.

The only 'currency' that God is concerned about is **"FAITH"** defined as *"faith which is motivated by LOVE" (Galatians 5:6)* and *"Without FAITH it is IMPOSSIBLE to please Him" (Hebrews 11:6).* God is not impressed by your race, title, and certainly not money. According to Jesus in the New Testament, *"the flesh profitteth nothing" (John 6:63).* And as Paul the Apostle said, *"Flesh and blood CANNOT inherit the Kingdom of God" (1 Corinthians 15:50).* Also, Paul, in giving his background as an "Israelite" said he counted his Jewish/Benjamin pedigree as *"dung" (Philippians 3:8).*

Finally we come to the end of this trail of clues to the Identity of Gog:

1. Gog is Agag, King of Edom/Amalek—*Numbers 24:7* —Septuagint and Jewish 'sages'
2. Gog/Agag/Edom disappeared into Jewry beginning 126 BC—Josephus, *Antiquities of the Jews*
3. Gog/Edom becomes the 'King of the Jews' beginning with King Herod the Edomite
4. Gog/Jewry incorporates the "house of Togarmah" the Khazars—about 740 AD
5. Gog/Rothschild/Capitalism takes control of the world money system—1740s until today
6. Gog/Rothschild/Communism becomes "Prince/Dictator of Rosh/Russia"—November 7th, 1917

These **'6' Clues** seems to be a pretty appropriate number to end our trail of clues with, since the devil seems to like that number, with 666 being his very own ID. In the next chapter, we move on to show you how *Ezekiel 38* is unfolding in the world today.

SIX

Ezekiel 38 and Gog's Invasion

In the previous chapters we have nailed down the identity of Gog and his allies as the present day forces of the Rothschild-financed, Jewish-led, Zionist/Communist/Capitalist hordes and established the date of November 7th, 1917 as the day when Gog becomes the "prince of Rosh/Russia." Now we will delve into a point by point explanation of the entire prophecy of *Ezekiel* against Gog. The prophecy found in chapter *Ezekiel 38* and *39* will begin to yield its highly symbolic language and give you a few laughs as well, that is if you don't happen to be one of Gog's 'horses.'

The way that *Ezekiel 38* unfolds is twofold. First, it presents a graphic literal picture of the Gog/Zionist/Rothschild invasion of the physical land of Israel. Second, it gives a graphic, symbolic illustration of the Gog/Communist/Rothschild conquest of the Christian "mountains/kingdoms" of true Israel. This is the way God works, and is clearly manifest in the Old Testament rituals and sacrifices which were a type, or pattern of the spiritual things revealed in the

Ukrainian Christians slaughtered by communist Jews. The Jews killed approximately 65 million throughout the USSR. Where's the Steven Spielberg *"Swindler's List"* on this Holocaust?

New Testament. God illustrates his truths by giving us *"first that which is natural; and afterward that which is spiritual" (1 Corinthians 15:46)*. In this case, the invasion of the natural "mountains of Israel" and the invasion of the spiritual mountains of Israel are going on simultaneously. In the interpretation of this prophecy we will bounce back and forth between these two entities—so pay attention.

The prophecy from *Ezekiel* will be in Italics and the interpretation will follow.

> *[1] And the word of the LORD came unto me, saying,*
>
> *[2] Son of man, set thy face* ***against Gog****, the land of Magog, the prince of Rosh, Meshech and Tubal, and prophesy against him,*
>
> *[3] And say, Thus saith the Lord GOD; Behold I am*

> *against thee, O Gog, the **prince of Rosh, Meshech** and **Tubal**:*

We are to prophesy "**Against** Gog" not "**Bless** Gog" which is what the majority of Christians are doing when they support Gog and his allies in this invasion of "the mountains of Israel." The "mountains" are both in the physical land of Israel and are the Christianized kingdoms of TRUE Israel which are, or rather were, in many nations of the world.

In the last century, Gog has invaded all these formerly Christianized nations. Today, they are some of the most reprobate nations on the planet. Did you know that when Gog and his Zionist/Edomite/Khazars began their invasion of the literal land of Israel that over 25% of Palestinian Arabs were Christians and that they were driven out of their homes and off the land? Did you know that when Gog and his Jewish/Communist/Khazars took over Christian Russia that they exterminated Christians by the tens of millions?

To clarify this a little further, there is NO such thing, nor has there ever been a truly 'Christian nation.' However, the nations that Gog has come against were "officially" Christian nations; they had adopted Christianity as their state religion. Russia was 'officially' a Christian nation and so were most of the European States. England is still 'officially' a Christian nation. Even the United States at one time, before the Jewish ACLU stepped in, considered itself an 'official' Christian nation. Jesus said His followers were to be "the salt of the Earth." Salt flavors and preserves. When Christians in a nation truly follow the Spirit of God they can flavor and preserve a nation. They can Christianize a nation by lifting up and influencing the nation's morals. But when they don't follow the Spirit, then you get the cesspool of the USA and Europe of today.

Mount Zion in the literal land of Israel was always supposed to **symbolize** the true spiritual/heavenly Mount Zion. Literal Jerusalem was only a symbolic picture of the *"heavenly Jerusalem."* Paul, in the Book of Hebrews, says, *"Ye are come (right now) to mount Sion and to the city of the living God, the heavenly Jerusalem" (Hebrews 12:22).* The ONLY way you can "ascend to the HILL of the Lord" is to have *"clean hands and a pure heart and not lift up your soul to vanity nor swear deceitfully" (Psalms 15* and *24).*

This is where the true "Mountain of Israel" is. These Mountains of Israel are all over the world. They are anywhere that followers of Christ are spiritually ascending Mount Zion, the Heavenly Jerusalem. These 'mountains' can be in China, Iran, Russia, USA, Mexico, Vietnam, etc. The chief enemy of these mountains, the enemy of Christians, is GOG! *Ezekiel 38* and *39* is ultimately about a war against Christianity, and Gog is leading the attack.

Colonel Jack Moore had an interesting analogy about all this: "What's happening today is almost a repeat, on a world scale, of the story of the good king Jehosophat and Ahab recorded in *2 Chronicles, chapters 18* and *19*. It is the story of a king of Judah named Jehosophat, who was seduced into helping an evil king of Israel named Ahab in a war that he was embarking on. [Much like the war evil leaders in Israel today are launching again in the Mid-East.]

Jehosophat told Ahab: *"My people will be as your people in this war" (2 Chronicles 18:3).* In the battle which followed, Ahab was killed, and Jehosophat escaped by the 'skin of his teeth.' When he returned to Jerusalem, he was met by a prophet of the Lord who told him: *"Shouldest thou help the ungodly? and love them, that hate the Lord? Therefore is wrath upon thee from before the Lord" (2 Chronicles 19:2).*

Maybe the Judeo-Christian preachers who praise the

antichrists of Judaism, calling them God's Chosen, should meditate on these words before they bring His Wrath on them and their people. If God never changes, as the Bible clearly teaches, then you need to consider this scripture: *"The wicked shall be turned into hell, and all the nations that forget God" (Psalms 9:10).*

How can Christian Americans spend a large portion of our Foreign Aid, giving "aid and comfort" to a people who hate our God, and hate everything we stand for as Christians?

> *And I will turn thee back, and put hooks into thy jaws, and I will bring thee forth, and all thine army, horses and horsemen, all of them clothed with all sorts of armour, even a great company with bucklers and shields, all of them handling swords (Ezekiel 38:4)*

God is going to lead Gog about as if he put "hooks in his jaws." These wicked 'Gogsters' think they are calling all the shots but God is using them as a threshing instrument to chastise his own people and bring them to repentance. As the Psalmist said, *"Deliver me from the wicked which is Thy (God's) sword" (Psalms 17:13).* And as the Lord says about the King of Assyria whom he sent against ancient Israel for their sins, *"O Assyrian, the rod of my anger, and the staff in their hand is mine indignation. I will send him against a hypocritical nation, and against the people of my wrath..." (Isaiah 10:5,6).* God raised up the Assyrian to judge and chastise his own people and God is still the same today.

The Bible says, *"When a man's ways please the Lord he makes even his enemies to be at peace with him" (Proverbs 16:7).* Why do you think God is raising up Gog and his army to come against the kingdoms/mountains of Israel? Because they need a lot of pruning and have a lot of issues that aren't pleasing to God, would be my guess. And that's why Gog has been able to do what he has done and why the former Christianized nations like the USA and Britain now have ZOG/GOG governments (Z.O.G. = Zionist Occupied Government).

All these "horses and shields and swords and armour" *(Ezekiel 38:4)*, definitely symbolize war—but they are very tricky guys, these Zionist children of Agag. When they first show up you don't see the sword until it's too late.

"The words of his mouth were smoother than butter, but war was in his heart, his words were softer than oil, yet were they drawn swords" (Psalms 55:21). All they want is 'civil rights' and 'peace'—a piece of this, a piece of that and they want you to be 'civil' when they steal it from you too! The "war" that Gog wages most effectively is a War of Words, a War of Propaganda! Remember, the Devil is the *"Father of Lies" (John 8:44)*. Lies are his most powerful weapon.

The GOG/communists come peaceably. *"Oh we just want to farm a little Kibbutz and grow a few vegetables and raise a few chickens for our chicken noodle penicillin soup."* That's how Gog came in to Palestine. That's the way Gog conquered Russia. Do you think Lenin got up on the weeks before the commies took over Russia and told the people: *"We are going to kill everyone that doesn't agree with the party line, and put hundreds of thousands of you into slave labor camps and burn down all the churches and drive this entire country into total paranoia where every other person is an informant."* Do you think that's what he promised the people? Or did he give 'em the ol' sleight of hand shuffle of "CHANGE!" and "TRUST ME!" and "YES WE CAN!?"

What kind of "horses" do you think these Khazar/Ashkenazis are galloping into Israel on? Well, since the

"There shall be a bridle in the jaws of the people causing them to err" (Isaiah 30:28).

Talmud says that the "Goyim are really beasts in human form" and are "like horses," I think they are riding in on the backs of "USEFUL IDIOTS," as Lenin called them, who are even now serving them: like John Hagee, and Hal Lindsey, and Pat Robertson and Tim Lahaye, the late Paul Crouch, and Chuck

Smith and just about every evangelical Christian out there, and let's not forget the Pope and the Catholic Church. They are the dumb horses and mules that are giving these children of Gog their 'horsey ride' in to possess the "mountains of Israel" both over there in the Mideast and throughout the world. They are even dumber than Baalam's ass who at least got his voice back to forbid the *"madness of the prophet" (2 Peter 2:16)* who was going the wrong way.

But no, these guys are not even in the same league as Baalam's ASS! Instead of warning the people they are just like *"dumb dogs that cannot bark" (Isaiah 56:10)*—which must be why they have D.D. after their name! They think they are fulfilling scripture in supporting Zionism, but really they are fulfilling the scripture that says, *"Be ye not as the horse or as the mule which have NO understanding whose mouth must be held in with bit and bridle lest it come nigh unto thee" (Psalms 32:9).*

Well, the "bit and bridle" has come "NIGH unto them" and it is in their mouth and the reins are in the hands of their master GOG. Why? Because "they have no understanding" of who Gog is and because the love of money has blinded their eyes—And most of all *"because of fear of the Jews" (John 19:38).*

These dumb clucks support their equally blind "beastly" governments in their slavish fealty to Jewish money-power. I will go as far as to say that without this blind support of churchianity towards Zionism, Gog would never have been able to pull off the heist of the world.

> *[5] Persia, Ethiopia, and Libya with them; all of them with shield and helmet:*

> *[6] Gomer, and all his bands; the house of Togarmah of the north quarters, and all his bands:*

and many people with thee.

[7] Be thou prepared, and prepare for thyself, thou, and all thy company that are assembled unto thee, and be thou a guard unto them.

"Persia, Ethiopia, Libya and Gomer"—These are the Jews coming out of these countries making "Aliyah," the Jewish term for the supposed "return" to Israel. The Jews from Persia are called Parsim Jews (Which in Hebrew means "Persians"). In the Mideast, Persian (Iranian) Jews form the largest community of Jews outside of Israel.

The black Ethiopian Jews, are called the Fallasha, the Mizrahim Jews came from Yemen, the Sephardi from Libya. Gomer is the area the East European Askenazi come out of. In 1949 and 1950, 30,000 Libyan Jews immigrated to Israel. After the 6-day war, about 22,000 from Ethiopia came in two onslaughts with 14,325 coming in one day in 34 aircraft. Persian/Iran sent another wave of 30,000 after the Khomeini Islamic revolution in 1979, and so it goes, all these Jewish 'bands' or groups coming out of those countries to 'return' to Israel.

The 'Shield' of Gog's army.

ALL have SHIELDS because they are financed by ROTHSCHILD which means RED SHIELD. Red Shield/ Lord Rothschild was the one to whom the Balfour Declaration was addressed, and Red Shield is the one who had financed the Lenin and Trotsky, Bolshevik/Commie revolution in Russia. And Red Shield and his money is the 'protection' for this whole army. Red Shield/Rothschild is the physical manifestation of GOG. He's the one who is to *"be thou a GUARD unto them" (v.7)*, a SHIELD of protection to this alien army. This army is still on the move and its key tactic is DECEPTION! It's all shielded and guarded and hidden until they have power, then the trap is sprung and you are in it.

> *[8] After many days thou shalt be visited: in the latter years thou shalt come into the land that is brought back from the sword, and is gathered out of many people, against the mountains of Israel, which have been always waste: but it is brought forth out of the nations, and they shall dwell safely all of them*

This is something the Prophet sees happening far in the future *"after many days"* in *"the latter years"* and *"in the latter days" (vs.16)*. The prophecy is telling you it is the 'latter days and latter years.' Because the prophecy is being fulfilled now.

To be *"brought back from the sword"* is another way of saying "the war is over." The world had just come out of the waste and desolation of World War I, which is why they "dwell safely all of them." All of this really got started at the end of World War I which was called "the war to end all wars." It caused a great false sense of security to fall on much of the world. This is brought out in chapter 39 of *Ezekiel* which says their "dwelling safely" was an illusion because the enemy was at the gate. The "Great War" had ended and all the world was finally at peace. The Mountains of Israel had just been brought out of the nations at war, and all was at rest.

Yet the enemy was at the gate, Gog was on the march with his army of deception!

Israel's Apartheid Wall

Dimensions of The Wall:

- 216 miles long
- 25 feet tall
- 95-315 feet of buffer zone with electric fences, trenches, cameras, and security patrol
- Three times as long and twice as high as the Berlin Wall.

God says in *Ezekiel 39* this period of "dwelling safely" was the very period when they were trespassing against God and is the reason He allowed the sword of Gog to come against them. It was *"because they trespassed against Me, therefore hid I my face from them, and gave them into the hand of their enemies (GOG): so fell they all by the sword...all their trespasses whereby they have trespassed against Me, when they dwelt safely in their land, and none made them afraid" (Ezekiel 39:23,26).*

When the Russian Czar fell and Orthodox Christianity succumbed to Gog's forces, it was because of their sins, their trespasses against God. When America falls it will be for the same reason. The forces of Gog are still 'riding' the dumb "horses and mules" of churchianity and avaricious 'Gentile' governments in the United States and throughout the world, but once they have achieved their goal of world domination, Gog will endeavor to slaughter those dumb beasts and feed them to the pigs. They won't 'eat them' (use them) because they are 'unclean' animals. According to *Leviticus,* horse meat is not Kosher.

> *[9] Thou shalt ascend and come like a storm, thou shalt be like a cloud to cover the land, thou, and all thy bands, and many people with thee.*

The Hebrew word used here for *"ascend,"* is ***"alah."*** This is the word that ***"Aliyah"*** is derived from. (See *Strong's Concordance* #5927 and #5944) When the Zionist followers of Gog say they want to 'return' to the *"mountains of Israel"* they say, **"We are making Aliyah."** It literally means "to go up" or "to ascend." The Israelis have made it part of the **"Law of Return,"** open to every person worldwide who supposedly is a Jew. I say 'supposedly' because Jesus said, *"I know the lies of those who say they are Jews and are not but are the synagogue of Satan" (Revelation 2:9).* The irony is that every time a Jew says they are making Aliyah to Israel they are actually fulfilling the prophecy of *Ezekiel 38:9*. They are the **"ascending/Aliyah" army of GOG!**

The Lord gives another analogy as to the *modus operandi* of Gog. Here He portrays Gog's forces to be like a *storm cloud that covers the land.* That would blot out all the light. What this represents is how Gog "covers" everything that he does so he hopes no one will figure it out, and it won't come to the light of day. In a word, it is deception. It is like the motto of the Israeli Gestapo, the Mossad: "Through deception make war." It is the way Gog operates. The entire Rothschild banking industry is based on deception. When the disciples asked Jesus what would be the sign of His coming and of the end of the world, the first words out of His mouth were: *"Take heed that no man deceive you" (Matthew 24:4).* He repeats that warning five different times in that discourse in *Matthew, chapter 24*. Over and over and over and over and over again, He warns about the deception that will occur just before His return. This "storm cloud" is when they blow the smoke of deception in your eyes, the smoke of the "BOTTOMLESS

ALIYAH: Gog's army "ascends…like a storm…against the mountains of Israel" (Ezekiel 38:9-11). Everytime a Gogster says they are making "Aliyah" to Israel, they are literally fulfilling Ezekiel's prophecy! They think "an evil thought…and say I will ascend…and go up to the land of unwalled villages" (Ezekiel 38:9-11). It is derived from the elements 'aliyah' meaning ascent and 'alah' to ascend, to go up. Aliyah is a war of immigration.

PIT" where all these "locusts" come from *(Revelation 9:1,2)*.

Ezekiel 38 goes on to state:

> *[10] Thus saith the Lord GOD; It shall also come to pass, that at the same time shall things come into thy mind, and thou shalt think an evil thought:*
>
> *[11] And thou shalt say, I will go up to the land of unwalled villages; I will go to them that are at rest, that dwell safely, all of them dwelling without walls, and having neither bars nor gates."*

Gog's army comes against *"**unwalled** villages"* which have *"neither bars or gates."* In 1948, when the Khazars came to the newly founded "Israel" enmasse, they met little resistance in Palestine, the "land of unwalled" villages. But Israel today is the most walled up, barred up and gated up place in the world. Besides the Apartheid Wall, and every other Israeli walking around with a machine gun, all the illegal Zionist settlements in the occupied territories are walled and gated up like miniature fortresses. This invasion began back in 1917 and escalated in 1948 when the Khazar Jews came against totally defenseless Palestine and when they took over the financial capitals of the world by deception and by stealth.

The phrase *"go up"* is from the same Hebrew word that *"ascend"* is translated from: *"Alah."* This word, as we showed above, is where the word ***"Aliyah"*** derives. This is the *"Aliyah"* of the Khazar and other false Jews as they go up like storm troopers to steal what was not theirs and never was theirs. God says that the *"evil thought"* is this ***"Aliyah"*** to go up like a cloud, covering your real intentions, like thieves to plunder those who are unprotected and at rest.

1.7 million American families lost their homes to foreclosure in 2007, 2.3 million in 2008, and 3.5 million in 2009. Meanwhile, billions of your tax dollars subsidize illegal Israeli apartheid colonies.

Gog comes against the "land of unwalled villages." But Israel today is the most walled up, fortified nation on the planet. All the settlements are walled and guarded. Even the "Israel Only" roads that criss-cross the land are walled off with fences, guard towers and land barriers. The Zionists were the ones that came against the "unwalled villages" beginning in the late 1800s with the main 'invasion' taking place after the Balfour Declaration to Lord Gog Rothschild on November 2, 1917.

This is ***literally*** what happened to the *Arabs* dwelling in *Palestine* when the Zionists came. The British and their allies had just delivered the land from the sword, defeating the Germans and the Turks in WWI. It was under British rule and protection. The Zionist immigrates to Palestine instead of coming in as friends and neighbors to the Arabs already living there, waged a war of immigration to displace the existing population and take over the country. It was never their intention to live in peaceful coexistence with their neighbors, *but in the beginning especially, they concealed this fact.*

But it didn't take long for the Arabs living in Palestine to figure out that these ***Zionists*** were *not coming in peace* but to *piecemeal* take all the land they could by any means. The Rothschild-financed Jewish National Fund began buying up land from mostly absentee Turkish landlords and tossing the Arab peasants off land that had been in their family for centuries. Any land acquired by the Fund had the stipulation that it was never to return to Arab possession.

Almost all of the land was ALREADY owned by the local inhabitants. By *1947* Jews only owned 6% of the land and only comprised one third of the population of Palestine. But through behind-the-scenes political maneuverings, pressures were brought on various countries, after WW2 and the United Nations 'partitioned the land' in November 1947. Yet the UN Partition plan granted the Jewish state 55% of the total land area. The Palestinian Arab state was to have an overwhelmingly Arab population, while the Jewish state would have almost as many Arabs as Jews. If it was unjust to force Jews to be a 1/3 minority in an Arab state, it was no more just to force Arabs to be an almost 50% minority in a Jewish state.

> The Palestinians rejected partition. The Zionists accepted it, but in private Zionist leaders had more expansive goals. In 1938, during earlier partition proposals, David Ben Gurion (first Israeli Prime Minister) stated, "when we become a strong power after the establishment of the state, we will abolish partition and spread throughout all of Palestine" (Noam Chomsky, *Fateful Triangle: The United States, Israel and the Palestinians*, updated edition, Cambridge: South End Press, 1999, p. 169n10).

On May 15, 1948 when Israel declared it's independence, it was well armed by the British, French and the Americans. It had made secret deals with Jordan to let it have the West Bank. Meanwhile, the Arabs were totally divided among themselves. The main reason King Farouk of Egypt sent in troops was as much to stop Jordan from expanding its territory as it was to defeat the Jews. From the Jews' perspective, the '48 war was not defensive but aggressive, it was to expand the territory given it by the Partition and to totally neutralize the proposed Palestinian state. In 1937, Ben Gurion had written to his son, *"We will expel the Arabs and take their places ... with the force at our disposal."* (Jerome Slater, *"What Went Wrong? The Collapse of the Israeli-Palestinian Peace Process," Political Science Quarterly, vol. 116, no. 2, 2001 p.173-174).*

The Israeli state, in fact, was founded in 1948 on the *forced expulsion of 700,000 Palestinians from their homeland.* 531 Arab villages were destroyed or depopulated. Hundreds of these emptied Arab villages were renamed and repopulated with Jews; this prompted Israeli Prime Minister Golda Meir to say years later: "How can we return the occupied territories? There is nobody to return them to."

Israeli Defense Forces (IDF) and militias committed a number of massacres in order to terrorize Palestinians into fleeing their homes. The most well-known being that of Deir Yassin in April, 1948, where Jewish paramilitary forces—the Stern Gang, the Haganah, and the Irgun led by Menachem Begin, who later became Prime Minister, slaughtered 250 men, women, and children. But there were many others, including the massacre of October 29, 1948, in which Israeli soldiers murdered 80-100 men, women, and children from the village Dawayma in the Haifa sub-district.

Israel's first Prime Minister, David Ben Gurion, is on record as saying: *"If I were an Arab leader, I would never sign an agreement with Israel. It is normal; we have taken their country. It is true God promised it to us, [no He didn't] but how could that interest them? Our God is not theirs. There has been Anti-Semitism, the Nazis, Hitler, Auschwitz, but was that their fault? They see but one thing: we have come and we have stolen their country. Why would they accept that?"* (Nahum Goldmann in *Le Paraddoxe Juif* (*The Jewish Paradox*, p. 121).

This policy of coming into the land like a *snake* and taking the land by subterfuge was first laid out by the founder of Zionism, Theodore Herzl, *"Spirit the penniless population across the frontier by denying it employment... Both the process of expropriation and the removal of the poor must be carried out discreetly and circumspectly."* (Theodore Herzl, founder of the World Zionist Organization, speaking of the Arabs of Palestine, *Complete Diaries*, June 12, 1895 entry.) Herzl's words contradict the oft-repeated Israeli lie that the Palestinians all showed up in Israel AFTER the Jews arrived in order to seek employment with the Jews. How do you know when these guys are lying? When they open their mouth and start talking!

The policy continued with Chaim Weizmann, *"We will establish ourselves in Palestine whether you like it or not... You can hasten our arrival or you can equally retard it. It is however better for you to help us so as to avoid our constructive powers being turned into a destructive power which will overthrow the world"* (Chaim Weizmann, Published in *"Judische Rundschau,"* No. 4, 1920). That may have referred to the power of Rothschild money when Weizmann made that threat but today it is even more ominous. Because today, Israel is thought to have around 400 nuclear missiles and bombs and have said if it looks like they are being defeated in a war would employ what they call the **"Samson Option"** and pull the whole world down on them in a nuclear holocaust. These guys are fanatical and crazy enough to do it, too!

A favorite, and oft repeated lie concocted by the Zionist propagandist, Israel Zangwill, in 1901 about Palestine was that it was *"a country without people for a people without a country."* The problem was that the land was not at all empty.

John Chancellor, the British high commissioner in Palestine, in the 1920s reported that "all cultivable land was occupied, [and] that NO cultivable land now in possession of the indigenous population could be sold to Jews without creating a class of landless Arab cultivators." All means all. The land was occupied and passed down to children for centuries. And contrary to Jewish myth, even before modern irrigation methods, it was the Palestinian farmers who were already making the "desert blossom like a rose" *(Isaiah 35:1).*

The British Mandate "Survey of Palestine" report of 1944-45 showed that the Palestinian farmers were producing 92% of Palestine grain, 86% of its grapes, 99% of its olives, 77% of its vegetables, 95% of its melons, 99% of its tobacco, and 60% of its bananas! Just think what they could have done, if they had the multi-billions funneled into the state every year by worldwide Jewry and ZOG/GOG nations.

The military of the USA and European nations are the dumb horses the Gogsters are using to ride to power on.

Since 1967, the US has disbursed more than

$200 billion dollars in unconditional financial and military aid to Israel, while offering blanket political support that allows Israel to do as it pleases. Britain, whose foreign policy is a carbon copy of Washington's, also supplies military hardware that goes directly to the West Bank and Gaza to facilitate the killing of Palestinians.

No state has received anywhere near as much foreign aid as Israel and no state has defied the international community on so many issues for so long. Then these crazy evangelicals set up their 'Christian' TV stations in Israel and beam the 'good news' about how wonderful Israel is to the Arabs. I picture Jesus taking a whip to them as he did to the money-changers in the Temple, only this will be at His return when *"they shall be BEATEN with many stripes" (Luke 12:47).*

The method that the Zionists have used to take over the literal land of Israel is no different than the way the Rothschilds have established a stranglehold on the world's financial system and are now in almost complete control of the most powerful governments on Earth. *Zionism, Capitalism and Communism* (the 3-legged 'Golem' monster of the Jews) are all based on deception and grow out of a mentality of racial superiority that is rooted in the Talmud.

Gog's Golem armies come...(Ezekiel 38)

> *[12] To take a spoil, and to take a prey; to turn thine hand upon the desolate places that are now inhabited, and upon the people that are gathered out of the nations, which have gotten cattle and goods, that dwell in the midst of the land.*
>
> *[13] Sheba, and Dedan, and the merchants of Tarshish, with all the young lions thereof, shall say unto thee, Art thou come to take a spoil? hast thou*

> *gathered thy company to take a prey? to carry away silver and gold, to take away cattle and goods, to take a great spoil?*

Six times in these two verses it spells out the *economic policy of the Zionists*: *"to take spoil... to take prey... silver... gold... cattle and goods."* Five times "take" is translated from the Hebrew "bazaz" meaning "to seize or plunder." I thought, 'well, that fits.' But, one time, "take" is translated from the Hebrew word meaning "to receive"... "silver and gold... cattle and goods." I thought, 'how does that fit?' But then it dawned on me 'boy, if that doesn't describe a Talmudic mentality, nothing does!' They operate from a principal that what the "goyim" have is actually theirs and when they steal from you they are not actually stealing but just 'receiving' what was already theirs in the first place. As Jesus said, *"they make the laws of God of none effect by their (Talmudic) traditions" (Mark 7:13).*

"*Sheba and Dedan,*" are the Saudis, and *"Tarshish"* and her *"young lions"* is Britain and the nations that come out of her. These are the "young lions" of the USA, Canada, Australia, etc. They are all wise to the shenanigans of these Zionists/ Gogsters and that's why they ask the question: "Are you come to take/plunder a spoil." But that's ALL they do, just question. They don't stop it, because their governments are so tied down by Rothschild banking money and Jewish-controlled media they are completely impotent to do anything.

As Ariel Sharon (Israeli war criminal) said, *"Every time we do something you (Shimon Peres) tell me America will do this and will do that... I want to tell you something very clear: Don't worry about American pressure on Israel. We, the Jewish people, control America, and the Americans know it." (Israeli Prime Minister, Ariel Sharon, October 3, 2001, to*

Shimon Peres, as reported on Kol Yisrael radio).

The Gogsters come against *"the people that are gathered out of the nations."* Some scriptural illiterates believe this is referring to the Jews who come from out of all the nations to make "Aliyah" to Israel. NO! They do come out of the nations but only as part of Gog's army as shown above. This is referring to the **British Mandate** over Palestine which carved the land area "out of the (former) nations" who had control of it before WW1. It had been made "desolate" through the 'Great War' but in 1922 the victorious allies carved up the entire Middle East into new geographical zones governed by them.

In an allegorical sense, this also refers to all the Christianized "Mountains/Kingdoms of true Israel" whose citizens are literally *"gathered out of the nations"* of the world. Just take a look at the 'melting pots' of the USA, and Canada. Gog has invaded these "kingdoms of true Israel" in the last century and has turned these former Christianized countries into antichrist cesspools. How did this happen? Because they thought "I am rich and increased with goods, and have need of nothing" but were really *"wretched and miserable and poor and blind and naked" Revelation 3:17).* So says Jesus Christ in the Book of Revelation about the Laodicean Church of western churchianity who thought they were "dwelling safely" *(Ezekiel 39:26)*—when really the barbarian antichrists of Gog were at the gate.

> *[14] Therefore, son of man, prophesy and say unto Gog, Thus saith the Lord GOD; In that day when my people of Israel dwelleth safely, shalt thou not know it?*
>
> *[15] And thou shalt come from thy place out of the north parts, thou, and many people with thee, all of*

them riding upon horses, a great company, and a mighty army:

[16] And thou shalt come up against my people of Israel, as a cloud to cover the land; it shall be in the latter days, and I will bring thee against my land, that the heathen may know me, when I shall be sanctified in thee, O Gog, before their eyes.

[17] Thus saith the Lord GOD; Art thou he of whom I have spoken in old time by my servants the prophets of Israel, which prophesied in those days many years that I would bring thee against them?

One thing we need to get straight in our heads is WHO is really "Israel" and WHO is really a "Jew." This is what the *"Controversy of Zion" (Isaiah 34:8)* is all about (see Appendix 1 following this chapter for an in depth treatment on this subject.)

The invasion of Palestine by Gog is just a type, just an illustration of what Gog is doing worldwide against the true Israel of God, the Christian believers. This is the worldwide war against Christianity by Gog. It has been going on for centuries, but this particular *"latter years"* war was originally launched "out of the north parts." Most of the original founders of Zionism, the Askenazi Jews, were from the north, from Eastern Europe. Millions of these invaders have come from Russia itself and about half of them are in the USA—and you wonder why the USA is so screwed up?

This IS the WAR of the Antichrist against the Church and the WHOLE world! As the Apostle Paul said, "The Jews… are contrary to ALL men!" (1 Thessalonians 2:14,15).

The only definition of the Antichrist in the ENTIRE Bible is given in the epistles of John: *"Who is a liar but he that denies that Jesus is the Christ? He is Antichrist that denies the Father and the Son, Whosoever denies the Son the same hath not the Father...this is a deceiver and an Antichrist" (1 John 2:22 & 4:3; 2 John 7)*. Who do you think that is talking about?

Who in the official literature of their religion says that "Jesus Christ was born of a whore?" And that, "He is even now in Hell suffering eternally in boiling excrement?" It certainly isn't in the Muslim Koran but it is in the Jewish Talmud. It is an absolute deception to think that little Antichrist state in the middle-east is the Israel of God. To believe that, is an absolute deception of Satan.

So what I'm telling you is that the so-called Israeli state is NOT Israel as far as God and His Word are concerned. Remember when we showed you back in chapter one that Esau/Edom became part of Jewry in 126 BC and that Edom disappeared into Jewry and became 'Jews' at that time? Well, guess where Edom is today? The Edomites are in Israel! They have assumed the names of Judah/Jew and Israel just like Ezekiel predicted they would.

Seir is another name for Edom *(Genesis 36:8)*. The Lord tells Ezekiel *"Son of man set thy face against mount Seir and prophesy against it... Because thou (Seir/Edom) hast said these two nations (Israel and Judah) and these two countries shall be mine and we will possess it" Ezekiel 35:2,10)*. Well, they have possessed both these names today. These Edomites are, in fact, *"Jews, who killed the Lord Jesus and their own prophets and are contrary to all men" (1 Thessalonians 2:14,15)*. Those who killed the King of Israel, the Lion of the tribe of Judah, have so befuddled churchianity that they think these Christ-killers are the chosen people.

You've heard of "identity theft?" Well, that's what the Israeli state is. It is identity theft to the max.

[18] And it shall come to pass at the same time when Gog shall come against the land of Israel, saith the Lord GOD, that my fury shall come up in my face.

The prophet Zechariah predicted that, *"The city (Jerusalem) shall be taken and the women ravished and the houses rifled, and half of the city shall go forth into captivity..... THEN shall the Lord go forth to fight against those Nations" (Zechariah 14:2,3).*

The ones who "took Jerusalem" are the Jews in the 1967 6-Day War. They are the ones who "rifled/robbed the houses and ravished the women!"

By 2001, according to the *Report of the Violation of Human Rights in Palestine*, half the Palestinian population of the Occupied Territories lived in refugee camps (John Dugard, Kamal Hossain, and Richard Falk, S-5/1 of 19 October 2000, E/CN.4/2001/121, 16 March 2001, para 29).

The Zionists/Gogsters are the ones who took the city, stole the houses, raped the women and drove half the indigenous population into the captivity of refugee camps. The Zionists/ Gogsters are the ones who came "against the land of Israel"— "against My people" the tens of thousands of Christian Palestinian Arabs living there, that the Gogsters killed, raped and drove into captivity.

But God is going to **lower the boom on them!**

[19] For in my jealousy and in the fire of my wrath have I spoken, Surely in that day there shall be a great shaking in the land of Israel;

[20] So that the fishes of the sea, and the fowls of the heaven, and the beasts of the field, and all creeping things that creep upon the earth, and all the men that are upon the face of the earth, shall shake at my presence, and the mountains shall be thrown down, and the steep places shall fall, and every wall shall fall to the ground.

[21] And I will call for a sword against him throughout all my mountains, saith the Lord GOD: every man's sword shall be against his brother.

[22] And I will plead against him with pestilence and with blood; and I will rain upon him, and upon his bands, and upon the many people that are with him, an overflowing rain, and great hailstones, fire, and brimstone.

[23] Thus will I magnify myself, and sanctify myself; and I will be known in the eyes of many nations, and they shall know that I am the LORD.

Throughout the **Old Testament** this is called the *"day of the Lord's vengeance;"* the *"great day of the Lord's wrath"* and the *"great and terrible day of the Lord."* In the **New Testament**: *"The day of our Lord Jesus Christ... when the Lord Jesus shall be revealed from heaven... in flaming fire taking vengeance upon them that know not God" (1 Corinthians 1:8 and 2 Thessalonians 1:7,8).*

At the coming of the Lord, the "overcomers" in Christ of all ages will be resurrected and receive glorified immortal bodies and shall reign on the Earth and in Heaven with Christ *(Revelation 20:4).*

This will be a terrible time when the *"cities of the nations fall" (Revelation 16:19)*, but also a time when *"healing waters" (Ezekiel 47:6-9)*, shall go out from the Lord *"for the healing of the nations" (Revelation 22:2)*.

From that day and forward the nations shall know God, that *"I am the Lord"* and the *"knowledge of the glory of the Lord shall cover the Earth as the waters cover the sea" (Habakkuk 2:14)*. For *"the Lord alone shall be exalted in that day" (Isaiah 2:11,17)*.

The turning of *"every man's sword against his brother"* happened several times in the Old Testament when the Lord sent His Spirit or an angel into the ranks of the enemy and they all went crazy and started killing each other. (See *Judges 7:22* and *1 Samuel 14:20*) One of the facets of the revelation of God is the *"TERROR of the Lord" (2 Corinthians 5:11)* It will be an absolute freak-out for those that have rejected the truth, and when it happens they will go absolutely insane.

Now we hop to the next chapter in Ezekiel, *Ezekiel 39:*

> *[1] Therefore, thou son of man, **prophesy against Gog**, and say, Thus saith the Lord GOD; Behold, **I am against thee, O Gog**, the prince of Rosh, Meshech and Tubal:*
>
> *[2] And I will turn thee back, and leave but the sixth part of thee, and will cause thee to come up from the north parts, and will bring thee upon the mountains of Israel:*

This chapter enlarges upon the destruction that God will bring upon Gog and why he allowed Gog to come against the "mountains of Israel" and what happens after Gog's destruction.

The word *"leave" (v. 2)* makes it appear to read that God

will *spare the "sixth part"* of Gog's army. This has caused some to think God would destroy all but 1/6th of Gog's army but this doesn't seem to fit *verse 4* which says God will destroy *"thee (Gog) and ALL thy bands."* But in the olde King James English sense of the word "leave" also means "give." In other words God will give Gog six parts. This "sixth part" according to *Matthew Henry's Commentary* are the six plagues or judgments of the previous chapter: *"pestilence, blood, overflowing rain, hailstones, fire and brimstone," (Ezekiel 38:22)*—God is going to wipe Gog out.

The ***"north parts"*** has some interesting symbolism. In many other prophecies it is associated with Babylon. In the book of Jeremiah, the Prophet said Babylon was the *"great evil from the north and a great destruction" (Jeremiah 4:6)*. In the book of *Zechariah* it symbolized the corruption of Zion from it's association with Babylon. *"Flee from the land of the north... deliver thyself O Zion that dwellest with the daughter of Babylon" (Zechariah 2:6,7).* Of course the preeminent people associated with Babylon today are the Jews with their Babylonian Talmud. They are "Babylon the Great, Mother of harlots"—the ***"harlots"*** being the churches of Judeo-Churchianity.

Also, **Israeli mercenaries**, known as the **US military**, have conquered modern Babylon (Iraq) for Israel. This is helping the state of Israel fulfill its dream of Greater Israel (Eretz Israel) which they believe is having all the land from the Nile river in Egypt to the Euphrates River in Iraq which used to be called Babylon.

Did you ever notice the two blue horizontal stripes on the Israeli flag? Do you know what they symbolize? The top blue stripe is the **Euphrates** river and the bottom blue stripe is the **Nile** river.

In *Daniel* chapter two in the Old Testament, the future of

The Israeli Flag: The top blue line represents the Euphrates River, the bottom line, the Nile River. The Zionists claim all the land in between. The main reason for all the wars in the Middle East is to help Israel get all this land through conquest.

world government from Babylon till today is envisioned as an idol with head of gold; breast and arms of silver; belly and thighs of brass; legs of iron and feet of iron and clay. It represents the successive kingdoms of Babylon, Medo-Persia, Greece, Rome and finally a ten nation confederacy of iron and clay. It is standing there when it is finally destroyed by a stone that smashes it on its feet—which represents the **return of Jesus Christ** to destroy worldly governments and set up His reign upon the Earth.

The image is from a dream given to King Nebuchadnezzar of Babylon and interpreted by the prophet Daniel around 600 BC. After the dream, the 3rd chapter of *Daniel* tells how the king set up a gigantic 60 by 6 cubit image, obviously based on this dream, and demands all to worship it. It says he set it up on the plain of ***"Dura."*** Dura means ***"circle"*** and it looks like world government has come full-circle back to Babylon.

It seems ironic that modern spiritual Babylon, as manifested in GOG/USA/Israel, has conquered literal physical Babylon, which today of course is called Baghdad

and Iraq. The USA is there to control the oil and help fulfill the Zionist dream of "Eretz Israel" as envisioned by it's founder, Gog. But ultimately it is there to fulfill the vision of *Daniel, chapter two* and it's destruction at the return of Christ who smashes the image on the *"toes of the feet"* as the prophecy says—*"Then was the iron, the clay, the brass, the silver, and the gold broken to pieces together and became as the chaff of the summer threshing floor and the wind carried them away: that no place was found for them: and the stone which hit the image became a great mountain and filled all the earth" (Daniel 2:31-45).* In *Ezekiel*, we read:

> *[3] And I will smite thy bow out of thy left hand, and will cause thine arrows to fall out of thy right hand.*
>
> *[4] Thou shalt fall upon the mountains of Israel, thou, and all thy bands, and the people that is with thee: I will give thee unto the ravenous birds of every sort, and to the beasts of the field to be devoured.*
>
> *[5] Thou shalt fall upon the open field: for I have spoken it, saith the Lord GOD.*
>
> *[6] And I will send a* ***fire on Magog****, and among them that dwell carelessly in the isles: and they shall know that I am the LORD.*
>
> *[7] So will I make my holy name known in the midst of my people Israel; and I will not let them pollute my holy name any more: and the heathen shall know that I am the LORD, the Holy One in Israel.*

These " bows" and "arrows" are weapons but not guns and missiles. In the New Testament we find that Gog will be *"consumed by the Spirit of His (Jesus') mouth and destroyed by the brightness of His coming" (2 Thessalonians 2:8), "by the sword which proceeded out of His mouth" (Revelation 19:21).* Isaiah prophesied of this day *"for My sword shall be bathed in heaven it shall come down upon Idumea, and upon the people of my curse, to judgment"* and there shall be *"a great sacrifice in the land of Idumea" (Isaiah 34:5,6).* The "land of Idumea" is the so-called nation of Israel. Idumea is the Greek word for Edom and "Edom is IN Jewry."

Not only will the sword of the Lord come against the Gogsters in the literal land of Israel but He will search them out all over the world and *"send a **fire** upon **Magog**"* wherever he tries to hide himself.

God calls in the beasts and carrion birds to clean up the mess. This *"great sacrifice"* the Revelation calls *"the supper of the great God, to eat the flesh of Kings... captains... mighty men... horses and them that sit upon them and all men both free and bond... small and great" (Revelation 19:17,18)* and let's not forget the banksters.

Gods chosen people, ***"Israel,"*** who are the believers in Christ, will not be allowed to *"pollute"* God's name anymore with their crazy doctrines (like thinking the Jews are the 'chosen people') and monetized churchianity.

> *[8] Behold, it is come, and it is done, saith the Lord GOD; this is the day whereof I have spoken.*
>
> *[9] And they that dwell in the cities of Israel shall go forth, and shall set on fire and burn the weapons, both the shields and the bucklers, the bows and the arrows, and the handstaves, and the spears, and*

they shall burn them with fire seven years:

[10] So that they shall take no wood out of the field, neither cut down any out of the forests; for they shall burn the weapons with fire: and they shall spoil those that spoiled them, and rob those that robbed them, saith the Lord GOD.

This is the *"great day of God's Wrath"* spoken of by all the prophets throughout the Bible.

I believe the *"Weapons... the shields... bucklers... the bows... the arrows... the handstaves... and the spears"* are not symbolic of any modern-day weapons—because how do you burn guns and tanks with fire? No, these weapons are the weapons that Gog used in a war of ideology. They are the lies and deceit and the propaganda with which he waged war on the minds of the people.

There are literally whole universities and libraries full of millions and millions and millions of books full of lies and half-truths and absolute doctrines of devils that will have to be burnt! These are the lying word weapons that the scriptures so

Daniel's image of worldly government is standing in Babylon when it is destroyed by the stone that smashes it on the feet of iron and clay.

What's burning here is PAPER! It has been ground up, formed into logs and then sawn into wheels. It can be used in either fireplaces or to cook with. We don't want to waste the books, but use them for fuel.

often talk about. *"Their tongue is as an arrow shot out, it speaketh deceit" (Jeremiah 9:8).* They are *"sons of men whose teeth are spears and arrows, and their tongue a sharp sword" (Psalms 57:4).* Instead of God's truth they have lies as their *"shield and buckler" (Psalms 91:4), "Who sharpen their tongue like a sword, and bent their bows to shoot their arrows, even bitter words" (Psalms 64).*

The problem is they just don't only speak lies anymore, they write them down in trillions and trillions of books. Karl Marx is reputed to have said, "give me 26 lead soldiers and I will conquer the world," referring to the 26 letters of the alphabet and the movable lead type then used in the printing press.

When Christ comes to rule this Earth, one of the first things He's going to do is burn all these lying books. Maybe He will start off with Marx's writings! No—I take that back, it will be the Talmud I'm sure. Maybe it will be used as kindling for roasting a pig. Would that make it kosher?

It will literally be like the science fiction novel *Fahrenheit 451* (451 is the temperature which ignites paper), only this time it won't be fiction. Since the Lord doesn't want to waste anything, people can use them for fires in their house or for cooking. People are doing it already. Retirees in England are buying old books and burning them in their fireplace to keep warm. It's cheaper than coal! This will include almost all the libraries of every city and all the universities and colleges and all the theological seminaries, most of all the textbooks of every grade school and all the bookstores. Am I forgetting anything?—Oh yeah, you can toss in all that paper money. It will be a new day! Out with the old and in with the new! According to *Ezekiel:*

> *[11] And it shall come to pass in that day, that I will give unto Gog a place there of graves in Israel, the valley of the passengers on the east of the sea: and it shall stop the noses of the passengers: and there shall they bury Gog and all his multitude: and they shall call it The valley of Hamon-gog.*
>
> *[12] And seven months shall the house of Israel be burying of them, that they may cleanse the land.*
>
> *[13] Yea, all the people of the land shall bury them; and it shall be to them a renown the day that I shall be glorified, saith the Lord GOD.*
>
> *[14] And they shall sever out men of continual employment, passing through the land to bury with the passengers those that remain upon the face of the earth, to cleanse it: after the end of seven*

months shall they search.

[15] And the passengers that pass through the land, when any seeth a man's bone, then shall he set up a sign by it, till the buriers have buried it in the valley of Hamon-gog.

[16] And also the name of the city shall be Hamonah. Thus shall they cleanse the land.

All of this will literally happen in Israel. Gog has led some seven million invaders into the land and God will give them one big mass graveyard. That's an awful lot of burying with gravediggers employed continually for "seven months."

Scholars have suggested several valleys where this mass burial ground could be but I like the one east of the Dead Sea because that was the original land of Edom, that is where the Israelis belong since they are Edomites.

[17] And, thou son of man, thus saith the Lord GOD; Speak unto every feathered fowl, and to every beast of the field, Assemble yourselves, and come; gather yourselves on every side to my sacrifice that I do sacrifice for you, even a great sacrifice upon the mountains of Israel, that ye may eat flesh,

Gog's invaders could be buried just south and east of the Dead Sea in their original land of Edom.

and drink blood.

[18] Ye shall eat the flesh of the mighty, and drink the blood of the princes of the earth, of rams, of lambs, and of goats, of bullocks, all of them fatlings of Bashan.

[19] And ye shall eat fat till ye be full, and drink blood till ye be drunken, of my sacrifice which I have sacrificed for you.

[20] Thus ye shall be filled at my table with horses and chariots, with mighty men, and with all men of war, saith the Lord GOD.

Again this is exactly the same as *Revelation 19* where it is called *"the supper of the great God."* Symbolically, either *"you eat the flesh of the Son of Man and drink His blood"* or you will be eaten and beasts will eat your flesh. Eat or be eaten! Gog and his followers and all the enemies of Christ aren't just in Israel either, this will be a supper that is all over the planet: *"the slain of the Lord shall be at that day from one end of the Earth even unto the other end of the Earth" (Jeremiah 25:33).*

[21] And I will set my glory among the heathen, and all the heathen shall see my judgment that I have executed, and my hand that I have laid upon them.

[22] So the house of Israel shall know that I am the LORD their God from that day and forward.

[23] And the heathen shall know that the house of

Israel went into captivity for their iniquity: because they trespassed against me, therefore hid I my face from them, and gave them into the hand of their enemies: so fell they all by the sword.

[24] According to their uncleanness and according to their transgressions have I done unto them, and hid my face from them.

[25] Therefore thus saith the Lord GOD; Now will I bring again the captivity of Jacob, and have mercy upon the whole house of Israel, and will be jealous for my holy name;

Most people are pretty dull when it comes to knowing God, including Christians, who are the ONLY house of Israel according to the apostle Paul who calls the Christians *"the Israel of God" (Galatians 6:16)*. God has to wake them up with a little judgment like it says here where God "gave them into the hand of their enemies" and "into captivity" *(v.23, 28)* because of their sins. The Lord is the Judge and *"the Lord is known by the judgment which He executeth" (Psalms 9:16)*. In this case He is known by the judgment which He brings on Gog and his followers and it wakes up both the heathen unbelievers and His own children.

The reason the church is fallen is because they were trespassing against God, and their largely messed-up state was because they were actually living in GOG/ZOG/"captivity" because of their sins. It is ONLY *"from this day and forward"* that God says Christians will *"Know that I am the Lord."* It is going to take the return of Christ Himself in order to set things right!

Church history, including Catholic, Orthodox and later

Protestant, is largely one long sorry story of politics, corruption and wacky doctrines. The only bright spots throughout church history are found in individuals who truly followed Christ and His example of loving God with all your heart, soul and mind and your neighbor as yourself. These are the *"overcomers."* These are the ones who will rule and reign with Christ at His return, NOT the vast multitudes of nominal Christians who will still have quite a few more lessons to learn.

Like Old Testament Israel, that went into one captivity after another because of various idolatry, the New Testament Israel has followed the same pattern. The "captivity" of ancient Israel was when they were put into subjection to different nations mainly because they were worshipping the idols of those nations.

The final captivity, other than under Roman rule, of ancient Israel was their Babylonian exile, and New Testament Israel has had its Babylonian captivity as well. This began to happen as they fell under the sway of the Jews and their Babylonian Talmudic religion and MONEY/MEDIA EMPIRE and into Judeo-churchianity which is where they are today:

> *[26] After that they have borne their shame, and all their trespasses whereby they have trespassed against me, when they dwelt safely in their land, and none made them afraid.*
>
> *[27] When I have brought them again from the people, and gathered them out of their enemies' lands, and am sanctified in them in the sight of many nations;*
>
> *[28] Then shall they know that I am the LORD their God, which cause them to be led into captivity*

among the heathen: but I have gathered them unto their own land, and have left none of them any more there.

[29] Neither will I hide my face any more from them: for I have poured out my spirit upon the house of Israel, saith the Lord GOD.

These verses about ***"the land"*** *(v.26, 28)* are ultimately interpreted in the Church, which is not the building or the organization, but is made up of all the believers in Christ. But these people who are looking to that little chunk of land in the Mideast as the fulfillment of "the land" are like little kids who can't distinguish between a toy car and a real one. They think the little illustrated sermon of the Old Testament with its rituals, and symbolism, and literal land and city is the ultimate reality when it was only a rough shadow of the real spiritual truth that God was trying to get across to them.

Paul interprets the *symbolism of* ***"the land"*** for us in the Book of Hebrews. He says that even Abraham who was the first one given the *"promise of the land,"* lived in the literal land as though he were in a *"foreign country" (Hebrews 11:9)!* Why? Because Abraham was NOT looking for a physical land, but was really seeking a heavenly or spiritual land.

Paul then gives example after example of Old Testament believers who did the same thing as Abraham. He said that all these, through their faith and obedience to God: *"declare plainly that they seek a better country...that is an heavenly country, wherefore God is not ashamed to be called their God for He hath prepared for them a city... which has foundations whose builder and maker is God" (Hebrews 11:9,10, 14-16).*

This is the land that all the saved of all ages inherit. This land is union with God, for when you have that, then you *"inherit all things."* You become the ***"Children of God**..., for they shall inherit the EARTH and the Kingdom of Heaven" (Matthew 5:3,5,9)* as Jesus said. You get everything, you get the entire Earth and Heaven too, not just some funky little piece of real estate in the desert that is soon to be blown to pieces and turned into a mass burial ground for all the Gogsters!

From these two chapters of *Ezekiel 38 and 39*, it looks like most of the church will not realize 'what's up' until the return of Christ. Because it says *"Then (at the revelation of God to destroy Gog) shall they know that I am God."* But maybe a lot of them will wake up before that when God fully *"gives them into the hands of their enemies" (v.23,27).* Who are these Zionist-Jewish-Gogsters whom they have been worshipping as *"the chosen people"* by which they have been literally **worshipping the antichrist?** What will happen then?

Well, just look what happened in Soviet Russia when Gog took over that country and multiply that 7 times for what will happen when Gog takes over the entire world. This will be the *"abomination of desolation spoken of by Daniel the Prophet"* and *"then will be Great Tribulation, such as was not since the beginning of the world to this time, no nor ever shall be" (Matthew 24:21).*

Being *"gathered into their own land"* is the second coming of Christ to *"gather together his elect from the four winds from one end of the Earth to the other end of the Earth."* This is the **first resurrection of the dead** who are the overcomers of all ages. This is when they inherit an immortal *"flesh and bone" body (Luke 24:39)* just like Jesus had after his resurrection. These will live and reign with Christ both on Earth and in Heaven.

Not 'The End' but only 'The Beginning!'

APPENDIX ONE

Who is Your Mother?

In the early years of Christianity, there was a terrific struggle between Judaism and the new sect of Christianity. Each side tried to prove that only it was the legitimate heir, that it alone was the true Israel and that the other party was under the curse of God.

By 311 AD, with Emperor Constantine's "Edict of Toleration," when Christianity became Rome's top religion, Christianity was no longer a religion of largely Jewish believers as it had been in its advent when it was regarded as a sect of Judaism. Now, it was almost entirely non-Jewish. They had experienced a long and bitter battle with flesh Jews who had often been instigator in there persecution.

It was during this time of religious rivalry that Replacement Theology found its beginnings in Origen, a church father in the middle of the second century. Writing in response to the bitter and violent opposition of the Jew to Christianity, Origen's view was that even though God had done His best to reach physical Israel with the Gospel, when they rejected and killed Jesus, and persecuted and killed the Apostles, God just cut them all off and replaced Israel with a Gentile church.

Even though in practice, by the time of Origen, it was

largely a Gentile church and it did appear to the natural eye that a Gentile church had replaced Israel, Origen's concept of replacement is scripturally impossible. Why? Because, according to the Word there is NO such thing as a 'Gentile Church.' A 'Gentile Church' did not REPLACE a 'Jewish nation' because the Church COULD NOT replace Israel. The reason it is impossible for the Church to replace Israel is because the Church IS Israel and the Church IS Judah. The term "Jew" is a shortened form of Judean or Judahite. The Hebrew term is Yehudi, meaning "of Judah." The Greek term is Ioudeos, "Judean."

Here is a little history: There were originally 12 tribes in Israel, Judah was one of them. The name Israel sometimes referred to the Northern 10 tribes that were conquered by the Assyrians and removed from their land as captives in 722 BC. Sometimes Israel referred to everyone in all 12 tribes. At the time of Christ, the Jews of that day were often referred to as Israel or Israelites.

Paul called himself an Israelite twice: *(Romans 11:1 and 2 Corinthians 11:22)*. Jesus was from the tribe of Judah and the *"King of the Jews" (Matthew 2:2)*. God gave Him *"the THRONE of his father David... over the House of Jacob/ Israel" (Luke 1:32,33)*. Those in Israel who accepted Him as Messiah, as "the King that comes in the name of the Lord" were the ones that God made the New Covenant with, as prophesied in *Jeremiah 31:31*, saying: *"Behold, the day cometh, saith the Lord, when I will make a NEW COVENANT with the house of ISRAEL and with the house of JUDAH."*

How many Gentiles were sitting at the table of the 'Last Supper' when Jesus instituted the meal that was to be a sign of the NEW COVENANT in His BLOOD? Not one! The 120 that were in the "Upper Room" on the day of Pentecost when the New Covenant was 'sealed' by the gift of the Holy Spirit were all from the house of Israel. The 3,000 that accepted Jesus as the Messiah that day were all "Jews and Jewish converts"—Peter called them all "Men of ISRAEL" *(Acts 2:22)*.

The question is not: "When did the Church REPLACE Israel?," but "When was the Church NOT Israel?" And the obvious answer is that it was Israel and nothing but Jews from the beginning! The 120 in the upper room on the day of Pentecost and the 3000 converts didn't STOP being Jews and "Men of Israel" that day! On the day of Pentecost, in 33 AD, the river of God's Spirit stopped flowing through national Israel, and changed course to flow only through the Church. The Church was NOW the "Israel of God."

Saved Gentiles, whether they understood it theologically or not, became part of the TRUE Israel and they fell under the New Covenant. They did NOT become a convert to Pharisaical Judaism. Pharisaical Judaism (what's going on in the nation of so-called Israel and worldwide Rabbinical Judaism today) is the religion of the antichrist rebels. These rebels are the ones who *"by their (TALMUDIC) traditions made void the law of God" (Mark.7:13)*. They are the ones who said and still say to God *"We will NOT have this MAN (Jesus Christ) to reign over us" (Luke 19:14)*. These are the ones Jesus called *"Mine enemies" (Luke 19:27)*.

So what happens to those genetic Jews and men of Israel who refused to accept the sacrifice of the *"Lamb of God which taketh away the sin of the world" (John 1:29)?* They are excommunicated from the nation of Israel. *Leviticus 17:4* says those who reject God's sacrifice were to be *"cut off from the people."* So, in God's eyes, those Jews who rejected Jesus' sacrifice for sin, were cut off from being Jews and Israel. They may call themselves Jews and Israel but as far as God is concerned, they are not! *Revelation 2:9* and *3:9*, quoted below, backs that up. This is what Paul refers to in *Romans*, *chapter 11*, where he says the unbelieving Jews were **"cut off"** from the tree of the covenants and promises made to Israel and believing Gentiles were "grafted in."

The "New Covenant" or "New Testament" was made with the literal "Israel of God" in fulfillment of prophecy, just as God predicted through the mouth of his prophets. All the prophecies about the New Covenant were predicted to be made with the Israel of God. Check it out: *Isaiah 55:3; Jeremiah 31:31 and 50:4,5; Ezekiel; 37:15-27.*

In fact, if the New Covenant/New Testament was ONLY made with the physical house of Judah and Israel, what do you think that means to you? That means that if you, as a Christian, believe that you are NOT a Jew or part of the physical nation of Israel you are NOT under the New Covenant! You are not even saved. And you are still in your sins.

This is why Paul said to the Gentile believers in Rome: *"He is NOT a Jew which is one outwardly, Neither is that circumcision which is outward in the flesh, but he is a JEW which is one INWARDLY and circumcision is that of the heart in the SPIRIT" (Romans 2:28,29).* This is why Paul told the Gentiles of Philipi: *"We (notice the plural pronoun 'we') are the Circumcision which worship God in the Spirit and rejoice in Christ Jesus" (Philippians 3:4).*

This is why Paul said to the Gentiles of the region of Galatia: *"IF ye be Christ's THEN are ye Abraham's SEED and heirs according to the PROMISE" (Galatians 3:29).*

And why Paul said to the same Gentiles: *"Now WE brethren (you Gentiles and us Jews) even as Isaac was are CHILDREN of the PROMISE" (Galatians 4:28).* This is why Paul called these same Gentiles: *"the ISRAEL of GOD" (Galatians 6:16)* This is why Paul said *"They are NOT all Israel who are OF Israel. The children of the FLESH are NOT the Children of God."* ONLY *"the children of Promise are counted for the SEED" (Romans 9:6-8).*

If you don't understand any of the above about exactly who Israel is and who it isn't then take it from Jesus' own words in the Book of Revelation. *"I know the blasphemy of them which say they are Jews, and are NOT, but are of the synaGOGue of Satan. Behold, I will make them of the synaGOGue of Satan, which say they are Jews, and are NOT, but do LIE; behold I will make them to come and worship before thy feet, and to know that I have loved thee" (Revelation 2:9* and *3:9).* Do you get that? Who do you think that is talking about?

Before we go any further with this study we need to get one thing clear. A popular **false** teaching is that, since the physical Jews are supposedly God's Chosen people, the Church must be raptured into heaven so that God can renew His separate program with the genetic Jew. Now, I won't get into all the end-time lunacy this heresy has fostered, but I will cut it off at the root by saying this: Since there is no salvation apart from belief in Christ, so-called physical Jews cannot and will not be saved unless they INDIVIDUALLY repent, believe the Gospel, and are baptized into the Church by the Holy Spirit *(Acts 2:38).* In fact, only THEN do they become a Jew and a citizen of Israel!

In *Galatians 3:26-29* and *Romans 9:6-8,* Paul plainly stated that being a flesh descendant of Abraham does NOT save anyone. In fact, he goes the extra step of proclaiming that the ONLY true descendants of Abraham were those who "are Christ's" via spiritual regeneration. Therefore it is an absolute LIE that there are two separate people of God—the Christian Church and the physical nation of Israel. The covenantal privilege that national Israel enjoyed as the chosen people of God was ended when the Jewish leaders *"fill[ed] up... the measure of [their] fathers' guilt" (Matthew 23:32)* by rejecting and crucifying their own Messiah. Jesus was very explicit in stating that the "house" of Israel was left "desolate" *(Matthew 23:37-39),* and that the Kingdom would be taken from the Jews as a people and given to another people *(Matthew 8:10-12, 21:33-45, etc.).*

Paul called them "Israel after the FLESH" to denote the difference between false and true Israel who are born after, or by, the SPIRIT. According to the Law of Moses, Israel *"after the flesh"* is *"under the CURSE of God"* as recorded in the Book of *Deuteronomy (28:15-68).* And the Apostle Paul confirmed the curse in the New Testament: *"The Jews, which killed the Lord Jesus and their own Prophets and are contrary to all men, forbidding us to preach the Gospel unto the Gentiles that they might be saved, for the WRATH OF GOD is come upon them to the UTTERMOST" (1 Thessalonians 2:14-16).*

They are STILL under that Curse and Wrath! What is happening today in so-called 'Israel' is completely Antichrist and it is what will usher in the reign of the Antichrist. To support Israel "after the flesh" in their rebellion against God, is to support the Antichrist and to place your self under the SAME Curse and Wrath that God Himself has said in His own Word that He has placed them under. This is exactly what God said to King Jehoshaphat when he helped the ungodly Ahab: *"And Jehu the son of Hanani the seer went out to meet him, and said to King Jehoshaphat, Shouldest thou help the ungodly, and love them that hate the LORD? therefore is wrath upon thee from before the LORD" (2 Chronicles 19:2).*

Evangelical leaders have taken out full-page ads in national newspapers like *The New York Times* to voice their support of a nation that is officially antichrist. Antichrist? Yes, ANTICHRIST! *"Who is a liar but he that denieth that Jesus is the Christ? He is ANTICHRIST, that denieth the Father and the Son" (1 John 2:22).*

This places the U.S. under the wrath of God. Have you ever thought about how the United States of America has gone to hell in a hand-basket ever since they began to support that antichrist illegal state in the Middle East? That started back in 1948, and the U.S. has had nothing but problems ever since.

Next, let's look at the set of scriptures that are taken and twisted by 'end-time experts' such as Hal Lindsey, Tim LaHaye and all Zionist Christians in a vain effort to 'prove' that ALL of national Israel "after the flesh" is going to be saved in these last days. These scriptures are in *Romans, chapter 11, verses 25-27:*

> *[25] For I would not, brethren, that ye should be ignorant of this mystery, lest ye should be wise in your own conceits; that blindness in part is happened to Israel, until the fullness of the Gentiles be come in.*
>
> *[26] And **SO** all Israel shall be saved: as it is written, there shall come out of Sion the Deliverer, and shall turn away ungodliness from Jacob:*
>
> *[27] For this is my covenant unto them, when I shall take away their sins.*

Words are important. That's why you need to pay attention and understand that Paul uses the word **"SO"** in verse 26 and doesn't use the word "THEN." "And **SO** all Israel shall be saved." Here is the dictionary definition of "So." It means, "in the way or manner shown, stated or described." Paul does NOT use "then" which means, "at that time." Most Christians have been so brainwashed by dispensational delusion that they read into these scriptures something that isn't even there, they read it as if it says that at some future date after all the Gentiles come in to some supposed Gentile church, THEN ALL Israel shall be saved. That is exactly NOT what Paul is talking about here!! He is NOT talking about some FUTURE time when all Israel shall be saved. Rather Paul is showing HOW all Israel shall be saved and were even at that time being saved, because ONLY those of the "Promise" are counted as ALL Israel!

Only those who *"call on the name of the Lord are saved" (Romans 10:13)*. When he says in verse 26 that *"the Deliverer SHALL COME out of Sion,"* he was quoting an Old Testament prophecy from *Isaiah, chapter 59, verses 20, 21* which was future at the time Isaiah wrote it. But when Paul is quoting it here, Jesus the Deliverer had ALREADY come and had ALREADY ESTABLISHED what God said was "My covenant" and had ALREADY "taken away their sins" at the cross. Paul was NOT predicting the coming of some future Deliverer, or Jesus appearing to so-called 'Israel' at the end-time or after the supposed pre-tribulation Rapture. He was merely backing up his argument with a scripture that had ALREADY been fulfilled.

"All Israel" being saved includes all who are of Christ, both Gentile and national Israel. THINK about it! That is why he started his explanation of who Israel is with the statement: *"they are NOT ALL Israel who are OF Israel."* In other words, not all of Israel is saved, only those who have faith in the Deliverer, Jesus Christ. If we add the dictionary definition of "so" and Paul's scriptural definition of who Israel is, here is what Paul is saying in *Romans 11:26: "And SO (in the manner that I've been showing you throughout this entire epistle, those who call themselves "Israel" are not the "Israel of God." Only those who call on the Name of the Lord are) all Israel (such as the Gentile 'brethren' of Galatia who were 'the Israel of God') shall be saved."*

"Blindness in PART is happened unto Israel, until the fullness of the Gentiles be come in." There is a period after that verse because that was the END of Paul's explanation of HOW "All Israel" was being saved. But it wasn't big enough to stop the runaway madness of dispensational delusion that rammed it into the next verse in an effort to make Paul say what he was NOT saying! He was NOT saying that once all the Gentiles that are supposed to get saved, THEN all Israel shall be saved. He was saying, Natural Israel shall be partially blind UNTIL all the Gentiles that are destined for salvation get saved, then national Israel won't be blind anymore.

But guess what? Neither will anybody else! Because, at the coming of Jesus Christ, EVERYBODY is going to SEE who He is. No more 'Blindness' for ANYONE when GOD rips off ALL the blinders from EVERYONE'S EYES!

Also, have you ever thought about exactly what the "in" was that the Gentiles were coming into when Paul says "Until the fullness of the Gentiles be come IN?" The Gentiles come IN to the Kingdom of ISRAEL! They are grafted in to the "olive tree" of the "covenants and promises" given to Israel!

'National Israel' didn't have TOTAL blindness then because, as the Apostle James said, there were at that time *"thousands of Jews which believe" (Acts 21:20).*

There are still to this day 'national Jews' being saved. What Paul is doing here in *Romans chapters 9* to *11* is explaining to his Gentile/Roman audience why only a "PART" of flesh and blood Israel believed. They were wondering: "If this Gospel you're preaching is true, Paul, and if Jesus was from the Tribe of Judah as you said *(Hebrews 7:14),* and the Old Testament prophecies are all about Jesus as Messiah—How come most of 'national Israel' is not only rejecting the

Gospel but also persecuting Christians? How come most believers are Gentiles rather than Jews (natural Israel)?"

Paul tells them that it is not because the Gentiles are so spiritual that God has chosen them. It is because God had blinded the eyes of flesh and blood Israel because of their unbelief. Paul is making them realize it's all by the grace of God. He doesn't want them to get on some puffed-up pride trip thinking God chose them because of some Holy-roller, self-righteousness or racial superiority they thought they possessed. And Paul is, above all, NOT setting up some kind of delusional, dispensational time prophecy for the total salvation of ALL Children of the FLESH of Isaac, 'national false Israel,' who are NOT "all Israel!"

Paul compared the relationship between True Israel and False Israel to the relationship between Isaac and Ishmael; *"Even as then, he (Ishmael) that was born after the FLESH persecuted him (Isaac) that was born after the SPIRIT, even so is it NOW" (Galatians4:29)* Paul was aligning the Antichrist flesh and blood Jews of his day to "Ishmael" who was "born after the flesh." That's a direct echo of *Romans 9:8* where he says *"They which are the children of the FLESH, these are NOT the CHILDREN OF GOD." And these "children of the flesh"* didn't fade away in 70 AD with the destruction of the Temple. And they didn't fade away in 311 AD with the Edict of Toleration.

Just as in Jesus' parable of the tares and wheat, where both grow together until Harvest, both the false Israel and the true Israel are still here. Today we find that "Blindness in PART" is STILL happening to FLESH Israel; even so, today we find they are still "enemies of the Gospel." So, does that mean we are to hate them because they are enemies of Christ and the Gospel? Of course not! Jesus said "Love your enemies." But don't be so stupid as to think that your enemies are your friends. Don't be so blind that you see **"wolves in sheep's clothing"** as actual sheep. Wake up! And hear the scriptures! Rip off those dispensational, delusionally-colored glasses so you can see the truth of the Word.

Paul's model of interpreting the Old Testament stories often turned the story on its head. In the Old Testament characters, Ishmael and Isaac, and Esau and Jacob/Israel, the national Jews would have looked at themselves as the good guys in the story. They would have seen themselves as Isaac and Jacob. But Paul says, NO!—You are the bad guys, and these whom you call 'Gentile dogs' are now the children of the promise, children of Abraham, Isaac and Jacob. They are the TRUE Israel in the eyes of God: The "Israel of God."

In *Galatians*, Paul compares "flesh Israel" to Ishmael who is "rejected" and "cast out," and he compares the new, Gentile believers to Isaac, "the seed of PROMISE." In *Romans, chapter 9* Paul says *"NEITHER because they are the SEED of ABRAHAM are they all CHILDREN but in ISAAC shall thy SEED be CALLED.*

That is, they which are the CHILDREN of the FLESH, THESE are NOT the CHILDREN of GOD." He compares national Israel to the "seed of the flesh" or Ishmael as the believers in Jesus are to the "Seed of Promise" or "Isaac." Paul continues in *Romans 9* by comparing national Israel to another child of the FLESH: Esau. Esau, even though he was the firstborn son and heir apparent, is rejected, and instead, Jacob, whose name was changed to Israel, becomes the promised seed. *"As it is written Jacob have I Loved but Esau have I hated" (Romans 9:12).*

In summary: Paul takes these Old Testament stories of Ishmael and Isaac, and Esau and Jacob, and turns them basically upside down, showing us that national, so-called Israel is really like Ishmael and Esau and the new Gentile believers are like Isaac and Israel. He calls these Gentiles: *"Jews;" "The Circumcision;" "Abraham's Seed;" "Children of the Promise;"* and *"the Israel of God,"* who were *"grafted in to the olive tree of the promises and covenants"* that God made to Abraham and the patriarchs. So then, what happens to national so-called Israel? Well, Paul gives the answer: ***"CAST OUT** the **bondwoman** and her **son (Ishmael/National Israel)**, for the son of the bondwoman shall **NOT** be heir with the son of the **freewoman (Isaac/The Church)**" (Galations 3:30*).

It says in *Galatians, chapter 4* that Abraham had two wives: "Hagar," a "bond or slave woman," who gave him a son called "Ishmael," and "Sarah," a "freewoman"' who gave him "Isaac." Paul compared Hagar and her son to earthly, fleshly Jerusalem and the Old Covenant, and he compared Sarah and Isaac to the spiritual, heavenly Jerusalem and the New Covenant. Spiritual Jerusalem is the mother of all true Christians as Paul said in *Galatians 4, verse 26. "But Jerusalem which is above is free, which is mother of US ALL!*

This "bondwoman" or "slave woman" that is to be "CAST OUT," Paul said is *"Jerusalem which NOW is."* It was there 2000 years ago and is still NOW with us today. Hagar's "son" includes ALL those looking to earthly Jerusalem as their "MOTHER." If you look to Jerusalem in the Middle East and its antichrist Talmudic Judaism as your "Mother"—and you call yourself a Judeo-Christian, then YOU are like Ishmael, who was Hagar's son. You are NOT like Isaac, who was the "Promised seed."

Just so you don't get confused about whom I'm referring, I mean all Jewish Zionists and their supporters, the Christian Zionists, like our cover boy John Hagee and all those like him. God did it to them once before in 70 A.D. and He's about to do it again. So, I'm asking you the BIG question: WHO IS YOUR MOTHER?

APPENDIX TWO

Talmud Quotations

Benjamin Freedman, pictured here, wrote the following in 1954 for Dr. David Goldstein, LL.D. of Boston, Massachusetts, to explain the history of the Khazar Jews. Freedman, a Jew, was a convert to Christianity. Freedman was an 'insider' and knew what the scam was. Unlike so many of today's so-called Jewish converts to Christianity, he decided to follow Jesus and fight the "money changers." The following is his exposé. It was originally printed as a booklet with the title, *Facts are Facts*, from which the following is excerpted. Benjamin Freedman's writings can be found on the web.

Benjamin Freedman

"From the Birth of Jesus until this day there have never been recorded more vicious and vile libelous blasphemies of Jesus, or Christians and the Christian faith by anyone, anywhere or anytime than you will find between the covers of the infamous "63 books" which are "the legal code which forms the basis of Jewish religious law" as well as the "textbook used in the training of rabbis." The explicit and implicit irreligious character and implications of the contents of the Talmud will open your eyes as they have never been opened before. The Talmud reviles Jesus, Christians and the Christian faith as the priceless spiritual and cultural heritage of Christians has never been reviled before or since the Talmud was completed in the 5th century. You will have to excuse the foul, obscene, indecent, lewd and vile language you will see here as verbatim quotations from the official unabridged translation of the Talmud into English. Be prepared for a surprise.

In the year 1935 the international hierarchy of so-called or self-styled "Jews" for the first time in history published an official unabridged translation of the complete Talmud in the English language with complete footnotes. What possessed them to make this translation into English is one of the unsolved mysteries. It was probably done because so many so-called or self-styled "Jews" of the younger generation were unable to read the Talmud in the many ancient languages in which the original "63 books" of the Talmud were first composed by their authors in many lands between 200 B.C. and 500 A.D.

The international hierarchy of so-called or self-styled "Jews" selected the most learned scholars to make this official translation of the Talmud into English. These famous scholars also prepared official footnotes explaining unabridged translation of the Talmud into English where they were required. This official unabridged translation of the Talmud into English with the official footnotes was printed in London in 1935 by the Soncino Press. It has been always referred to as the Soncino Edition of the Talmud. A very limited number of the Soncino Edition were printed. They were not made available to any purchaser. The Soncino Edition of the Talmud is to be found in the Library of Congress and the New York Public Library. A set of the Soncino Edition of the Talmud has been available to me for many years. They have become rare "collector's items" by now.

The Soncino Edition of the Talmud with its footnotes is like a double-edged sword. It teaches the Talmud to countless millions of the younger generation of so-called or self-styled "Jews" who are not able to read the Talmud in the many ancient languages in which the Talmud was written by its authors between 200 B.C. and 500 A.D. It also teaches Christians what the Talmud has to say about Jesus, About Christians and about the Christian faith. Someday this is bound to back-fire. Christians will some day challenge the assertion that the Talmud is the "sort of book" from which Jesus allegedly "drew the teachings which enabled him to revolutionize the world" on "moral and religious subjects." The rumbling is already heard in places.

Verbatim quotations from the Soncino Edition of the Talmud are required to illustrate the enormity of the Talmud's iniquity. My comments with verbatim quotations will prove inadequate to do that. In spite of the low language I will of necessity therefore include in this letter to you I have no compunctions in the matter because the United States Post Office authorities do not bar the Soncino Edition of the Talmud from the mails. Nevertheless I apologize in advance for the language which will of necessity appear in this letter to you. You now understand.

The world's leading authorities on the Talmud confirm that the official unabridged Soncino Edition of the Talmud translated into English follows the original texts with great exactness. It is almost a word-for-word translation of the original texts. In his famous classic *"The History of the Talmud,"* Michael Rodkinson, the leading authority on the Talmud, in collaboration with the celebrated Reverend Dr. Isaac M. Wise states:

> "With the conclusion of the first volume of this work at the beginning of the twentieth century, we would invite the reader to take a glance over the past of the Talmud, in which he will see… that not only was the Talmud not destroyed, but was so saved that NOT A SINGLE LETTER OF IT IS MISSING; and now IT IS FLOURISHING TO SUCH A DEGREE AS CANNOT BE FOUND IN ITS PAST HISTORY… THE TALMUD IS ONE OF THE WONDERS OF THE WORLD. During the twenty centuries of its existence… IT SURVIVED IN ITS ENTIRETY, and not only has the power of its foes FAILED TO DESTROY EVEN A SINGLE LINE, but it has not even been able materially to weaken its influence for any length of time. IT STILL DOMINATES THE MINDS OF A WHOLE PEOPLE, WHO VENERATE ITS CONTENTS AS DIVINE TRUTH... The colleges for the study of the Talmud are increasing almost in every place where Israel dwells, especially in this country where millions are gathered for the funds of the two colleges, the Hebrew Union College of Cincinnati and the Jewish Theological Seminary of America in New York, in which the chief study is the Talmud... There are also in our city houses of learning (Jeshibath) for the study of the

> Talmud in the lower East Side, where many young men are studying the Talmud every day."

This "divine truth" which "a whole people venerate" of which "not a single letter of it is missing" and today "is flourishing to such a degree as cannot be found in its history" is illustrated by the additional verbatim quotations which follow:

In order not to leave any loose ends on the subject of the Talmud's reference to Jesus, to Christians and to the Christian faith I will below summarize translations into English from the Latin texts of Rev. Pranaitis' *"The Talmud Unmasked, The Secret Rabbinical Teachings Concerning Christians."* It would require too much space to quote these passages verbatim with their foot-notes from the Soncino Edition in English.

First I will summarize the references by Rev. Pranaitis referring to Jesus in the Talmud in the original texts translated by him into Latin, and from Latin into English:

Sanhedrin, 67a — Jesus referred to as the son of Pandira, a soldier.

Kallah, 1b. (18b) — Illegitimate and conceived during menstruation.

[Editors Note: The Talmud actually brags about the Jews killing Jesus Christ, they don't let the Romans take credit for it." According to the Talmud, Jesus was executed by a proper rabbinical court for idolatry, inciting other Jews to idolatry, and contempt of rabbinical authority. All classical Jewish sources which mention his execution are quite happy to take responsibility for it; in the Talmudic account the Romans are not even mentioned."—Dr. Israel Shahak, *Jewish History, Jewish Religion*, pp. 97- 98, 118.]

Sanhedrin, 43a — On the eve of Passover they hanged Jesus.

Sanhedrin, 67a — Hanged on the eve of Passover. Toldath Jeschu. Birth related in most shameful expressions

Sanhedrin, 103a. — Suggested corrupts his morals and dishonors self.

Sanhedrin, 107b. — Seduced, corrupted and destroyed Israel.

Zohar (III, 282) — Died like a beast and buried in animal's dirt heap.

Hilkoth Melakhim — Attempted to prove Christians err in worship of Jesus

Abhodah Zarah, 21a — Reference to worship of Jesus in homes unwanted.

Orach Chaiim, 113 — Avoid appearance of paying respect to Jesus.

Iore dea, 150,2 — Do not appear to pay respect to Jesus by accident.

Abhodah Zarah (6a) — False teachings to worship on first day of Sabbath

Gittin 57a. — Says Jesus is in hell, being boiled in "hot excrement."

The above are a few selected from a very complicated arrangement in which many references are obscured by intricate reasoning. The following are a few summarized references to Christians and the Christian faith although not always expressed in exactly that manner. There are eleven names used in the Talmud for non-Talmud followers, by which Christians are meant. Besides Nostrim, from Jesus the Nazarene, Christians are called by all the names used in the Talmud to designate all non-"Jews": Minim, Edom, Abhodan Zarah, Akum. Obhde Elilim, Nokrim, Amme Haarets, Kuthim, Apikorosim, and Goim. Besides supplying the names by which Christians are called in the Talmud, the passages quoted below indicate what kind of people the Talmud pictures the Christians to be, and what the Talmud says about the religious worship of Christians:

Hilkhoth Maakhaloth — Christians are idolators, must not associate.
Abhodah Zarah (22a) — Do not associate with gentiles, they shed blood.
Iore Dea (153, 2) — Must not associate with Christians, shed blood.
Abhodah Zarah (25b) — Beware of Christians when walking abroad with them.
Orach Chaiim (20, 2) — Christians disguise themselves to kill Jews.
Abhodah Zarah (15b) — Suggest Christians have sex relations with animals.
Abhodah Zarah (22a) — Suspect Christians of intercourse with animals.
Schabbath (145b) — Christians unclean because they eat accordingly
Abhodah Zarah (22b) — Christians unclean because they not at Mount Sinai.
Iore Dea (198, 48) — Clean female Jews contaminated meeting Christians.
Kerithuth (6b p. 78) — Jews called men, Christians not called men.
Makkoth (7b) — Innocent of murder if intent was to kill Christian.
Orach Chaiim(225, 10) — Christians and animals grouped for comparisons.
Midrasch Talpioth 225 — Christians created to minister to Jews always.
Orach Chaiim 57, 6a — Christians to be pitied more than

sick pigs.

Zohar (II, 64b) — Christian idolators likened to cows and asses.

Kethuboth (110b) — Psalmist compares Christians to unclean beasts.

Sanhedrin (74b). Tos. — Sexual intercourse of Christian like that of beast.

Kethuboth (3b) — The seed of Christian is valued as seed of beast.

Kidduschim (68a) — Christians like the people of an ass.

Eben Haezar (44,8) — Marriages between Christian and Jews null.

Zohar (II, 64b) — Christian birth rate must be diminished materially.

Zohar (I, 28b) — Christian idolators children of Eve's serpent.

Zohar (I, 131a) — Idolatrous people (Christians) befoul the world.

Emek Haschanach (17a) — Non-Jews' souls come from death and death's shadow.

Zohar (I, 46b, 47a) — Souls of gentiles have unclean divine origins.

Rosch Haschanach (17a) — Non-Jews souls go down to hell.

Iore Dea (337, 1) — Replace dead Christians like lost cow or ass.

Iebhammoth (61a) — Jews called men, but not Christians called men.

Abhodah Zarah (14b) T — Forbidden to sell religious works to Christians

Abhodah Zarah (78) — Christian churches are places of idolatry.

Iore Dea (142, 10) — Must keep far away physically from

churches.

Iore Dea (142, 15) — Must not listen to church music or look at idols

Iore Dea (143, 1) — Must not rebuild homes destroyed near churches.

Hilkoth Abh. Zar (10b) — Jews must not resell broken chalices to Christians.

Chullin (91b) — Jews possess dignity even an angel cannot share.

Sanhedrin, 58b — To strike Israelite like slapping face of God.

Chagigah, 15b — A Jew considered good in spite of sins he commits.

Gittin (62a) — Jew stay away from Christian homes on holidays.

Choschen Ham. (26,1) — Jew must not sue before a Christian judge or laws.

Choschen Ham (34,19) — Christian or servant cannot become witnesses.

Iore Dea (112, 1) — Avoid eating with Christians, breeds familiarity.

Abhodah Zarah (35b) — Do not drink milk from a cow milked by Christian.

Iore dea (178, 1) — Never imitate customs of Christians, even hair-comb.

Abhodah Zarah (72b) — Wine touched by Christians must be thrown away.

Iore Dea (120, 1) — Bought-dishes from Christians must be thrown away.

Abhodah Zarah (2a) — For three days before Christian festivals, avoid all.

Abhodah Zarah (78c) — Festivals of followers of Jesus regarded as idolatry.

Iore Dea (139, 1) — Avoid things used by Christians in their worship.

Abhodah Zarah (14b) — Forbidden to sell Christians articles for worship.

Iore Dea (151,1) H. — Do not sell water to Christians articles for baptisms.

Abhodah Zarah (2a, 1) — Do not trade with Christians on their feast days.

Abhodah Zarah (1,2) — Now permitted to trade with Christians on such days.

Abhodah Zarah (2aT) — Trade with Christians because they have money to pay.

Iore Dea (148, 5) — If Christian is not devout, may send him gifts.

Hilkoth Akum (IX,2) — Send gifts to Christians only if they are irreligious.

Iore Dea (81,7 Ha) — Christian wet-nurses to be avoided because dangerous.

Iore Dea (153, 1 H) — Christian nurse will lead children to heresy.

Iore Dea (155,1) — Avoid Christian doctors not well known to neighbors.

Peaschim (25a) — Avoid medical help from idolators, Christians meant.

Iore Dea (156,1) — Avoid Christian barbers unless escorted by Jews.

Abhodah Zarah (26a) — Avoid Christian midwives as dangerous when alone.

Zohar (I, 25b) — Those who do good to Christians never rise when dead.

Hilkoth Akum (X,6) — Help needy Christians if it will promote peace.

Iore Dea (148, 12H) — Hide hatred for Christians at their

celebrations.

Abhodah Zarah (20a) — Never praise Christians lest it be believed true.

Iore Dea (151,14) — Not allowed to praise Christians to add to glory.

Hilkoth Akum (V, 12) — Quote Scriptures to forbid mention of Christian god.

Iore Dea (146, 15) — Refer to Christian religious articles with contempt.

Iore Dea (147,5) — Deride Christian religious articles without wishes.

Hilkoth Akum (X,5) — No gifts to Christians, gifts to converts.

Iore Dea (151,11) — Gifts forbidden to Christians, encourages friendship.

Iore Dea (335,43) — Exile for that Jew who sells farm to Christian.

Iore Dea (154,2) — Forbidden to teach a trade to a Christian

Babha Bathra (54b) — Christian property belongs to first person claiming.

Choschen Ham (183,7) — Keep what Christian overpays in error.

Choschen Ham (226,1) — Jew may keep lost property of Christian found by Jew.

Babha Kama (113b) — It is permitted to deceive Christians.

Choschen Ham (183,7) — Jews must divide what they overcharge Christians.

Choschen Ham (156,5) — Jews must not take Christian customers from Jews.

Iore Dea (157,2) H — May deceive Christians that believe Christian tenets.

Abhodah Zarah (54a) — Usury may be practiced upon Christians or apostates.

Iore Dea (159,1) — Usury permitted now for any reason to Christians.

Babha Kama (113a) — Jew may lie and perjure to condemn a Christian.

Babha Kama (113b) — Name of God not profaned when lying to Christians.

Kallah (1b, p.18) — Jew may perjure himself with a clear conscience.

Schabbouth Hag. (6d) — Jews may swear falsely by use of subterfuge wording.

Zohar (I, 160a) — Jews must always try to deceive Christians.

Iore Dea (158,1) — Do not cure Christians unless it makes enemies.

Orach Cahiim (330,2) — Do not assist Christian's childbirth on Saturday.

Choschen Ham (425,5) — Unless believes in Torah do not prevent his death.

Iore Dea (158,1) — Christians not enemies must not be saved either.

Hilkkoth Akum (X,1) — Do not save Christians in danger of death.

Choschen Ham (386,10) — A spy may be killed even before he confesses.

Abhodah Zorah (26b) — Apostates to be thrown into well, not rescued.

Choschen Ham (388,15) — Kill those who give Israelites' money to Christians

Sanhedrin (59a) — 'Prying into Jews' "Law" to get death penalty

Hilkhoth Akum (X,2) — Baptized Jews are to be put to death

Iore Dea (158,2) Hag. — Kill renegades who turn to Christian rituals.

Choschen Ham (425,5) — Those who do not believe in Torah are to be killed.

Hilkhoth tesch.III,8 — Christians and others deny the "Law" of the Torah.

Zohar (I, 25a) — Christians are to be destroyed as idolators.

Zohar (II, 19a) — Captivity of Jews end when Christian princes die.

Zohar (I, 219b) — Princes of Christians are idolators, must die.

Obadiam — When Rome is destroyed, Israel will be redeemed.

Abhodah Zarah (26b) T. — "Even the best of the Goim should be killed."

Sepher Or Israel 177b — If Jew kills Christian commits no sin.

Ialkut Simoni (245c) — Shedding blood of impious offers sacrifice to God.

Zohar (II, 43a) — Extermination of Christians necessary sacrifice.

Zohar (I, 38b,39a) — High place in heaven for those who kill idolators.

Hilkhoth Akum (X,1) — Make no agreements and show no mercy to Christians

Hilkhoth Akum (X,1) — Either turn them away from their idols or kill.

Hilkhoth Akum (X,7) — Allow no idolators to remain where Jews are strong.

Choschen Ham (388,16) — All contribute to expense of killing traitor.

Pesachim (49b) — No need of prayers while beheading on Sabbath.

Schabbath (118a) — Prayers to save from punishment of coming Messiah.

Weird and totally perverted sexual ideas and practices that are described in the Soncino Talmud follow here with the quotes taken directly from the Soncino Talmud.

SANHEDRIN, 55b: "A maiden three years and a day may be acquired in marriage by coition, and if her deceased husband's brother cohabits with her, she becomes his. The penalty of adultery may be incurred through her; (if a niddah) she defiles him who has connection with her, so that he in turn defiles that upon which he lies, as a garment which has lain upon (a person afflicted with gonorrhea)." (emphasis in original text of Soncino Edition, Ed.)

(footnotes) "(2) His wife derives no pleasure from this, and hence there is no cleaving. (3) A variant reading of this passage is: Is there anything permitted to a Jew which is forbidden to a heathen. Unnatural connection is permitted to a Jew. (4) By taking the two in conjunction, the latter as illustrating the former, we learn that the guilt of violating the injunction 'to his wife but not to his neighbor's wife' is incurred only for natural but not for unnatural intercourse." (emphasis in original, Ed.)

SANHEDRIN, 69a "'A man'; from this I know the law only with respect to a man: whence do I know it of one aged nine years and a day who is capable of intercourse? From the verse, And 'if a man'? (2) He replied: Such a minor can produce semen, but cannot beget therewith; for it is like the seed of cereals less than a third grown (3)."

(footnotes) (2) 'And' (') indicates an extension of the law, and is here interpreted to include a minor aged nine years and a day. (3) Such cereals contain seed, which if sown, however, will not grow."

SANHEDRIN, 69b "Our rabbis taught: If a woman sported lewdly with her young son (a minor), and he committed the first stage of cohabitation with her, -Beth Shammai say, he thereby renders her unfit for the priesthood (1). Beth Hillel declare her fit...All agree that the connection of a boy nine years and a day is a real connection; whilst that of one less than eight years is not (2); their dispute refers only to one who is eight years old.

(footnotes) (1) i.e., she becomes a harlot whom a priest may not marry (Lev XXL,7.). (2) so that if he was nine years and a day or more, Beth Hillel agree that she is invalidated from the priesthood; whilst if he was less than eight, Beth Shammai agree that she is not."

KETHUBOTH, 5b. "The question was asked: Is it allowed (15) to perform the first marital act on the Sabbath? (16). Is the blood (in the womb) stored up (17), or is it the result of a wound? (18).

(footnotes) "(15) Lit., 'how is it'? (16) When the intercourse could not take place before the Sabbath (Tosaf) (17) And the intercourse would be allowed, since the blood flows out of its own accord, no wound having been made. (18) Lit., or is it wounded? And the intercourse would be forbidden."

KETHUBOTH, 10a-10b. "Someone came before Rabban Gamaliel the son of Rabbi (and) said to him, 'my master I have had intercourse (with my newly wedded wife) and I have not found any blood (7). She (the wife) to him, 'My master, I am still a virgin.' He (then) said to them; Bring me two handmaids, one (who is) a virgin and one who had intercourse with a man. They brought to him (two such handmaids), and he placed them on a cask of wine. (In the case of) the one who was no more a virgin its smell (1) went through (2), (in the case of) the virgin the smell did not go through (3). He (then) placed this one (the young wife) also (on the cask of wine), and its smell (4) did not go through. He (then) said to him: Go, be happy with thy bargain (7). But he should have examined her from the beginning (8)."

(footnotes) "(1) i.e., the smell of wine. (2) One could smell the wine from the mouth (Rashi). (3) One could not smell the wine from the mouth. (4) i.e., the smell of wine. (5) Rabban Gamaliel (6) To the husband. (7) The test showed that the wife was a virgin. (8) Why did he first have to experiment with the two handmaids."

KETHUBOTH, 11a-11b. "Rabba said, It means (5) this: When a grown up man has intercourse with a little girl it is nothing, for when the girl is less than this (6), it is as if one puts the finger in the eye (7), but when a small boy has intercourse with a grown up woman, he makes her as 'a girl who is injured by a piece of wood.'"

(footnotes) "(5). Lit., 'says.' (6) Lit., 'here,' that is, less than three years old. (7) Tears come to the eyes again and again, so does virginity come back to the little girl under three years."

KETHUBOTH, 11a-11b. "Rab Judah said that Rab said: A small boy who has intercourse with a grown up woman makes her (as though she were) injured by a piece of wood (1). Although the intercourse of a small boy is not regarded as a sexual act, nevertheless the woman is injured by it as by a piece of wood."

(footnotes) "(1) Although the intercourse of a small boy is not regarded as a sexual act, nevertheless the woman is injured by it as by a piece of wood."

HAYORATH, 4a. "We learnt: (THE LAW CONCERNING THE MENSTRUANT OCCURS IN THE TORAH BUT IF A MAN HAS INTERCOURSE WITH A WOMAN THAT AWAITS A DAY CORRESPONDING TO A DAY HE IS EXEMPT. But why? Surely (the law concerning) a woman that awaits a day corresponding to a day is mentioned in the Scriptures: He hath made naked her fountain. But, surely it is written, (1)- They might rule that in the natural way even the first stage of contact is forbidden; and in an unnatural way, however, is (that the ruling might have been permitted) (3) even in the natural way (4) alleging (that the prohibition of) the first stage (5) has reference to a menstruant woman only (6). And if you prefer I might say: The ruling may have been that a woman is not regarded as a zabah (7) except during the daytime because it is written, all the days of her issue (8)." (emphasis appears in Soncino Edition original, Ed.)

(footnotes) "(13) Lev. XV, 28. (14) Cf. supra p. 17, n. 10. Since she is thus Biblically considered unclean how could a court rule that one having intercourse with her is exempt? (15) Lev XX, 18. (1) Ibid. 13. The plural "xxxx" (Hebrew characters, Ed.) implies natural, and unnatural intercourse. (2) Why then was the case of 'a woman who awaits a day corresponding to a day' given as an illustration when the case of a menstruant, already mentioned, would apply the same illustration. (3) The first stage of contact. (4) In the case of one 'who awaits a day corresponding to a day'; only consummation of coition being forbidden in her case. (5) Cf. Lev XX, 18. (6) Thus permitting a forbidden act which the Sadducees do not admit. (7) A woman who has an issue of blood not in the time of her menstruation, and is subject to certain laws of uncleanness and purification (Lev XV, 25ff). (8) Lev XV, 26. Emphasis being laid on days."

ABODAH ZARAH, 36b-37a. "R. Naham b. Isaac said: They decreed in connection with a heathen child that it would cause defilement by seminal emission (2) so that an Israelite child should not become accustomed to commit pederasty with it...From what age does a heathen child cause defilement by seminal emission? From the age of nine years and one day. (37a) for inasmuch as he is then capable of the sexual act he likewise defiles by emission. Rabina said: It is therefore to be concluded that a heathen girl (communicates defilement) from the age of three years and one day, for inasmuch as she is then capable of the sexual act she likewise defiles by a flux.

SOTAH, 26b. "R. Papa said: It excludes an animal, because there is not adultery in connection with an animal (4). Raba of Parazika (5) asked R. Ashi, Whence is the statement which the Rabbis made that there is no adultery in connection with an animal? Because it is written, Thou shalt not bring the hire of a harlot or the wages of a dog etc.; (6) and it has been taught: The hire of a dog (7) and the wages of a harlot (8) are permissible, as it is said, Even both of these (9) - the two (specified texts are abominations) but not four (10)...As lying with mankind. (12) But, said Raba, it excludes the case where he warned her against contact of the bodies (13). Abaye said to him, That is merely an obscene act (and not adultery), and did the All-Merciful prohibit (a wife to her husband) for an obscene act?" (emphasis in the original text, Ed.)

(footnotes) "(4) She would not be prohibited to her husband for such an act. (5) farausag near Baghdad v. BB. (Sonc. Ed.) p. 15, n.4. He is thus distinguished from the earlier Rabbi of that name. (6) Deut. XXIII, 19. (7) Money given by a man to a harlot to associate with his dog. Such an association is not legal adultery. (8) If a man had a female slave who was a harlot and he exchanged her for an animal, it could be offered. (9) Are an abomination unto the Lord (ibid). (10) Viz., the other two mentioned by the Rabbi. (11) In Num. V. 13. since the law applies to a man who is incapable. (12) Lev. XVIII, 22. The word for 'lying' is in the plural and is explained as denoting also unnatural intercourse. (13) With the other man, although there is no actual coition." (emphasis appears in original Soncino Edition, Ed.)

YEBAMOTH, 55b. "Raba said; for what purpose did the All-Merciful write 'carnally' in connection with the designated bondmaid (9), a married woman (10) and a sotah (11)? That in connection with the designated bondmaid (is required) as has just been explained (12). That in connection with a married woman excludes intercourse with a relaxed membrum (13). This is a satisfactory interpretation in accordance with the view of him who maintains that if one cohabited with forbidden relatives with relaxed membrum he is exonerated (14); what, however, can be said, according to him who maintains (that for such an act one is) guilty? The exclusion is rather that of intercourse with a dead woman (15). Since it might have been assumed that, as (a wife), even after her death, is described as his kin (16), one should be guilty for (intercourse with) her (as for that) with a married woman, hence we are taught (that one is exonerated).

(footnotes) (9) Lev. XIX,20. (10) Ibid. XVIII,20 (11) Num. V, 13. (12) SUPRA 55a. (13) Since no fertilization can possibly occur. (14) Shebu., 18a, Sanh. 55a (15) Even though she dies as a married woman. (16) In Lev. XXI, 2. where the text enumerates the dead relatives for whom a priest may defile himself. As was explained, supra 22b, his kin refers to one's wife." (emphasis in Soncino Edition original, Ed.)

YEBAMOTH, 103a-103b. "When the serpent copulated with Eve (14) with lust. The lust of the Israelites who stood at Mount Sinai (16) came to an end, the lust of idolators who did not stand at Mount Sinai did not come to an end."

(footnotes) "(14) In the Garden of Eden, according to tradition. (15) i.e., the human species. (16) And experienced the purifying influence of divine Revelation."

YEBAMOTH, 63a. "R. Eleazar further stated: What is meant by the Scriptural text, This is now bone of my bones, and flesh of my flesh (5)? This teaches that Adam had intercourse with every beast and animal but found no satisfaction until he cohabited with Eve.

(footnotes) "(5) Gen. II, 23. emphasis on This is now." (emphasis appears in original Sonsino Edition, Ed.)

YEBAMOTH, 60b. "As R. Joshua b. Levi related: 'There was a certain town in the Land of Israel the legitimacy of whose inhabitants was disputed, and Rabbi sent R. Ramanos who conducted an inquiry and found in it the daughter of a proselyte who was under the age of three years and one day (14), and Rabbi declared her eligible to live with a priest (15)."

(footnotes) "(13) A proselyte under the age of three years and one day may be married by a priest. (14) And was married to a priest. (15) i.e., permitted to continue to live with her husband."

YEBAMOTH, 59b. "R. Shimi b. Hiyya stated: A woman who had intercourse with a beast is eligible to marry a priest (4). Likewise it was taught: A woman who had intercourse with that which is no human being (5), though she is in consequence subject to the penalty of stoning (6), is nevertheless permitted to marry a priest (7).

(footnotes) "(4) Even a High Priest. The result of such intercourse being regarded as a mere wound, and the opinion that does not regard an accidentally injured hymen as a disqualification does not so regard such an intercourse either. (5) A beast. (6) If the offense was committed in the presence of witnesses after due warning. (7) In the absence of witnesses and warning."

YEBAMOTH, 12b "R. Bebai recited before R. Naham: Three (categories of) woman may (7) use an absorbent (8) in their marital intercourse (9), a minor, a pregnant woman and a nursing woman. The minor (10) because (otherwise) she might (11) become pregnant, and as a result (11) might die...And what is the age of such a minor? (14). From the age of eleven years and one day until the age of twelve years and one day. One who is under (15), or over this age (16) must carry on her marital intercourse in the usual manner."

(footnotes) "(7) (so Rashi. R. Tam; Should use, v.Tosaf s.v.) (8) Hackled wool or flax (9) To prevent conception (10) May use an absorbent. (11) Lit., 'perhaps'. (14) Who is capable of conception but exposed thereby to the danger of death. (15) When no conception is possible. (16) When pregnancy involves no fatal consequences."

YEBAMOTH, 59b. "When R. Dimi came (8) he related: It once happened at Haitalu (9) that while a young woman was sweeping the floor (10) a village dog (11) covered her from the rear (12) and Rabbi permitted her to marry a priest. Samuel said: Even a High Priest.

(footnotes) "(8) From Palestine to Babylon (9) (Babylonian form for Aitulu, modern Aiterun N.W. of Kadesh, v. S. Klein, Beitrage, p. 47). (10) Lit., 'house'. (11) Or 'big hunting dog' (Rashi), 'ferocious dog' (Jast.), 'small wild dog' (Aruk). (12) A case of unnatural intercourse.

KETHUBOTH, 6b. "Said he to him: Not like those Babylonians who are not skilled in moving aside. (7), but there are some who are skilled in moving aside (8). If so, why (give the reason of) 'anxious.? (10) - for one who is not skilled. (Then) let the[m] say: One who is skilled is allowed (to perform the first intercourse on Sabbath), one who is not skilled is forbidden? -Most (people) are skilled (11). Said Raba the son of R. Hanan to Abaye' If this were so, then why (have) groomsmen (12) why (have) a sheet? (13) - He (Abaye) said to him: There (the groomsmen and the sheet are necessary) perhaps he will see and destroy (the tokens of her virginity) (14).

(footnotes) "(7) i.e., having intercourse with a virgin without causing a bleeding. (8) Thus no blood need come out, and 'Let his head be cut off and let him not die!' does not apply. (9) If the bridegroom is skilled in 'moving sideways'. (10) He need not be anxious about the intercourse and should not be free from reading Shema' on account of such anxiety. (11) Therefor the principle regarding 'Let his head be cut off and let him not die!' does not, as a rule, apply. (12) The groomsmen testify in case of need to the virginity of the bride. V. infra 12a. If the bridegroom will act in a manner that will cause no bleeding, the groomsmen will not be able to testify on the question of virginity. (13) To provide evidence of the virginity of the bride. Cf. Deut. XXII,17. (14) It may happen that he will act in the normal manner and cause bleeding but he will destroy the tokens and maintain that the bride was not a virgin; for this reason the above mentioned provisions are necessary. Where however he moved aside and made a false charge as to her virginity, the bride can plead that she is still a virgin (Rashi)."

Then There is the Kol Nidre:

One of the handiest devices provided by the Talmudic "Sages" to offset Moses' laws against swearing falsely, is found in the Talmud book of Nedarim (Vows), and is put into practice yearly in every synagogue across the world as the "Kol Nidre" (all vows).

The text of the Kol Nidre may be found in the Jewish Encyclopedia. Three times the Cantor, to a tune that sounds like the melodious grief of all ages, pompously intones the words: "All vows, obligations, oaths ... whether called 'konam,' 'konas,' or by any other name, which we may vow or swear, or pledge, or whereby we may be bound, from this Day of Atonement until the next (whose happy coming we await), we do repent. May they be deemed absolved, forgiven, annulled, and void and made of no effect... The vows shall not be reckoned vows; the obligations shall not be obligatory; nor the oaths be oaths."

The confirming reply of the Congregation is typical of blasphemous Judaistic misuse of the Bible. Three times a verse from Numbers is chanted. It actually concerns the duty of a congregation which has violated the laws of God, in ignorance, to repent, and states:

> "And it shall be forgiven, all the congregation of Israel, and the stranger that sojourneth among them; seeing all the people were in ignorance."

Here is a typical Talmudic situation: Knowingly, in advance, every shred of truth is to be cast away, with religious support. A Scriptural verse of no relevance whatsoever is used as justification.

With the Jewish Kol Nidre, not only is there no repentance involved, as in the Bible itself, but forthright, blatant disavowal and annulment of solemn oaths an entire year in advance.

The text of the Kol Nidre also appears in the Talmud, Book of Nedarim, 23a. The Talmud Mishna states: "EVERY VOW WHICH I MAY MAKE IN THE FUTURE SHALL BE NULL. HIS VOWS ARE THEN INVALID PROVIDING

THAT HE REMEMBERS THIS AT THE TIME OF THE VOW." The Kol Nidre is repeated on the following page. Discounting the irrelevant "filler" about a man eating with his friend, we see in a footnote:

> "This may have provided support for the custom of reciting Kol Nidre (a formula for dispensation of vows) prior to the Evening Service of the Day of Atonement... But Kol Nidre as part of the ritual is later than the Talmud... [as] the law of revocation in advance was not made public."

However, this advance disavowal of oaths, and sanction of perjury, did become known at various times. *The Jewish Encyclopedia* account concerning Kol Nidre relates how this practice of revoking all vows to be made, a year in advance, was used in European countries to bar the oath of a Jew as of no value. Contemporaneously, however, as we have been in ignorance of the Kol Nidre and what it means, such oaths, no matter how valueless, are foolishly accepted in our Courts.

[Editor note: The bottom line is that these masters of deceit are now in control of the planet and have weaved a web of total deception to ensnare your mind. If you, as a so-called 'Christian' zionist, support these antichrist's you are as guilty as they are, only worse.]

FOR MORE INFORMATION ON THIS AND MANY OTHER FASCINATING TOPICS:

Power of Prophecy offers a free sample copy of his newsletter focusing on world events, false religions, secret societies, cults, and the occult challenge to Christianity. If you would like to receive this newsletter, please write to:

Power of Prophecy
4819 R. O. Drive, Suite 102
Spicewood, Texas 78669

You may also e-mail your request to:
customerservice1@texemarrs.com

FOR OUR WEBSITE

Power of Prophecy's monthly newsletter is published free on our website. This website has descriptions of all our books, and is packed with interesting, insight-filled articles, videos, breaking news, and other information. You also have the opportunity to order an exciting array of books, tapes, and videos through our online Catalog and Sales Store. Visit our website at:

www.powerofprophecy.com

OUR SHORTWAVE RADIO PROGRAM

Power of Prophecy's international radio program, *Power of Prophecy*, is broadcast weekly on shortwave radio throughout the United States and the world. *Power of Prophecy* can be heard on WWCR at 4.840 Sunday nights at 9:00 p.m. Central Time. You may also listen to *Power of Prophecy* 24/7 on our website *powerofprophecy.com*